Battleground Europe
ACCRINGTON PALS TRAIL

Other guides in the Battleground Europe Series:
Ypres - Hill 60 *by* Nigel Cave
Ypres - Sanctuary Wood and Hooge *by* Nigel Cave
Ypres - Passchendaele: The Fight for the Village *by* Nigel Cave
Ypres - Messines Ridge *by* Peter Oldham
Walking the Somme *by* Paul Reed
Somme - Serre *by* Jack Horsfall & Nigel Cave
Somme - Beaumont Hamel *by* Nigel Cave
Somme - Gommecourt *by* Nigel Cave
Somme - Thiepval *by* Michael Stedman
Somme - La Boisselle *by* Michael Stedman
Somme - Fricourt Mametz *by* Michael Stedman
Somme - Guillemont *by* Michael Stedman
Somme - Pozières *by* Graham Keech
Somme - Courcelette *by* Paul Reed

Arras - Vimy Ridge *by* Nigel Cave
Hindenburg Line *by* Peter Oldham

Battleground Europe Series guides in preparation:

Walking the Salient *by* Paul Reed
Ypres - Polygon Wood *by* Nigel Cave

Somme - Combles *by* Paul Reed
Somme - Delville Wood *by* Nigel Cave
Somme - Boom Ravine *by* Trevor Pigeon
Somme - Carnoy-Montauban *by* Graham Maddocks
Somme - High Wood *by* Terry Carter

Boer War - The Relief of Ladysmith, Colenso, Spion Kop *by* Lewis Childs
Boer War - The Siege of Ladysmith *by* Lewis Childs

Hindenburg Line - Cambrai: Right Hook *by* Jack Horsfall & Nigel Cave
Hindenburg Line - Epehy *by* Bill Mitchinson
Hindenburg Line - Riqueval *by* Bill Mitchinson

Battleground Europe

ACCRINGTON PALS TRAIL

William Turner

Series editor
Nigel Cave

LEO COOPER

First published in 1998 by
LEO COOPER
an imprint of
Pen Sword Books Limited
47 Church Street, Barnsley, South Yorkshire S70 2AS

ISBN 0 85052 636 1

A CIP catalogue of this book is available
from the British Library

Printed by Redwood Books Limited
Trowbridge, Wiltshire

*For up-to-date information on other titles produced under the Leo Cooper imprint,
please telephone or write to:*

Pen & Sword Books Ltd, FREEPOST, 47 Church Street
Barnsley, South Yorkshire S70 2AS
Telephone 01226 734222

CONTENTS

Foreword

For anyone like Bill Turner, to build upon a deservedly recognised achievement must be a satisfying experience. All those who have read and learned from Turner's 'Accrington Pals' and its supplement, 'The Accrington Pals Remembered', will welcome this guide book extension of his lovingly tended field of socio-military history. The author's books ensure that we know something of the local background of the men of the 11th Service Battalion of the East Lancashire Regiment, of their deeds, of the memorials of their collective service, and of where their fallen lie buried or simply commemorated. The reader of this new book will now be taken as a rather special 'pilgrim tourist' in the footsteps of the Accrington Pals on their wartime journeys, with periods in the line, in reserve and at rest, noting what still remains recognisable of what those Lancashire soldiers saw in the second decade of a century now ending.

The story is frequently told in the words of Pals having vivid powers of recall. By this means, on location in the United Kingdom, on troop transport, in Egypt and in France, we find ourselves with the Pals from the formation of the battalion and throughout its service until its last shots were fired.

We were with them on the Somme in front of Serre in July 1916, in Oppy Wood in 1917, again in July, and we learn in detail how Lieutenant Horsfall won his Victoria Cross at Ayette in March 1918. We are also introduced to a much more recent story, one of real fascination. Bill calls this 'the Pals Industry', and while one recognises the appropriateness of an image of 'labour', certainly Turner's labour, perhaps more appropriate might have been a word conveying the author's dedicated nurturing of society's indebtedness to those men of 1914. East Lancashire's debt is clearly established, but by extension, it is our debt too, wherever we may come from, a debt to a whole generation of men who, for a range of reasons, responded positively to their nation's call at a time of need.

Bill Turner's work, and that of others who have directed their attention towards locally raised units, has been invaluable. This local historian understands the wider scene within which his books are set and not least because of this, he has played a notable part in ensuring that 'his' Pals are understood as men of their time with the perception, values and attitudes of their time. From such an understanding, the respect in which the men of the 11th Service Battalion of the East Lancashire Regiment have always been held, is refurbished here. Turner has served them well.

Peter Liddle

Introduction

The placename 'Accrington' is of Saxon origin – 'the place of acorns'. From these pastoral days, Accrington, with a variety of spellings, in time became a village of hand-loom weavers, which in 1811 had just over 3,000 inhabitants. In common with many others in Lancashire, the village rapidly expanded throughout the Victorian era into an industrial town, which at the outbreak of war in 1914, had a population of some 45,000.

At that time Accrington was a centre of the Lancashire cotton weaving industry. In the town and in the surrounding small townships there were also calico printing works, collieries, brickworks, textile engineering works and iron foundries.

The whole area was a centre of heavy industry. For example, the industrial township of Church, with a population of 6,888 in an area of only 528 acres (214 hectares) had printing and dye works, iron foundries, cotton mills, collieries, naptha distilleries and chemical works within it's boundaries. (Thus Church, as a manufacturer of khaki and navy blue dyes, and, more deadly, as a manufacturer of nitric and picric acid, phosgene and explosives, was to make it's own particular contribution to the war effort).

Church, however, was but one of the several townships surrounding, and contiguous with, Accrington. Clayton-le-Moors, Oswaldtwistle, Rishton and Great Harwood, together with Church, were self-governing Urban District Councils. Each had a similar industrial base. Clayton-le-Moors had brickworks, cotton mills and calico printing; Oswaldtwistle had cotton mills, collieries and chemical works; Rishton had cotton mills, collieries and paper mills

The Leeds and Liverpool canal at Rishton. Victoria Mill on the left, Britannia Mill is on the right. *(Local Studies Library, Accrington.)*

and Great Harwood also had cotton mills and collieries. All were similar in population size, with Oswaldtwistle the largest at 15,717 (1911 census).

When the borough of Hyndburn (named after a local river) was formed in 1974, the Urban Districts, plus the Rural District of Altham, were included with Accrington. Hyndburn now covers over twenty-eight square miles (7,300 hectares) of north east Lancashire and has a total population of over 78,000.

In the minds of many people however, the Saxon 'Accrington' is synonymous with the red, iron-hard, 'Nori' Accrington brick, known world-wide for it's strength and impermeability (and used for this reason when the brickwork of the Thiepval Memorial arches was renewed in the 1980's). There is also 'Accrington Stanley' (1894-1961), one of the founding members of the Football League. 'Stanley' could never overcome the obstacle of having much wealthier clubs five miles either side of the town (Blackburn Rovers and Burnley). It took the death of the club to bring it fame – even cult status. (The new team now plays in the Unibond Premier League.)

One can add to these, of course, the 'Accrington Pals'. It must be said however, that the name is something of a misnomer. Although the Pals were formed in Accrington by the Mayor of Accrington, only one of the four original companies (250 men each) was of men originally from Accrington. A second, the 'District', was of men from the surrounding townships, the third from Chorley (with a Blackburn Detachment of fifty men), and the fourth from Burnley.

Workers at Martholme Colliery, Great Harwood. *(Local Studies Library, Accrington.)*

SCALE 1" = 9 miles

(MAPS COURTESY OF HYNDBURN BOROUGH COUNCIL)

HYNDBURN
Scale 1" = 3 miles

Weavers at York Mill, Rishton. *(Local Studies Library, Accrington)*

Although much of the textile and heavy engineering industry known to the Pals has gone, the Hyndburn area is still a thriving manufacturing centre. The Borough Council's initiatives over the years, of setting up business parks, has attracted many small – and not so small – manufacturing units and retail services. In Clayton-le-Moors (Altham) there are now corporate workwear, office furniture, sports goods and aircraft parts manufacturers and suppliers. Cotton weaving, chemical works and food producers employ many in Oswaldtwistle. Food products, light engineering and plastic products predominate in Great Harwood, with precision engineering and carpet manufacturing in nearby Rishton. Church has Hyndburn's largest employer of labour – a mail-order gifts distributor and greetings card manufacturer. Church however, still has chemical and engineering works.

The main employers in Accrington are as diverse as greetings cards manufacturers, brick works and makers of products for the car and aircraft industries. There are also many small firms producing or supplying a wide variety of products. The most significant change in the town from the days when the Pals was formed is the disappearance of the 'Globe' works of the textile engineering firm of Howard and Bulloughs. Here, in 1914, over 4,000 men and boys were employed, of whom quite a number enlisted in the Pals. The present-day 'Globe Centre', a five storey block where once cast-iron beams and machinery parts were made, is now a business resource and conference centre. Under the same roof is a restaurant, brasserie and a small hotel. This development alone illustrates the changes in Accrington since the days of the Pals.

Hyndburn, in the 1990's, has twice the national average (36%) of manufacturing industries and at 5.3% has a currently (1998) lower unemployment level than most towns in Great Britain. The life-style of it's citizens, reflected by the education, housing, travel, shopping and leisure facilities available, is another complete change to the days of poverty, social deprivation and industrial grime many of the Pals would know. The moorlands, the hills and the picturesque villages of east Lancashire were there then of course, only now the North West Tourist Board and Hyndburn Borough Council encourage visitors to discover and enjoy the area and its heritage.

The Accrington Pals are part of this heritage. Their story is not, however, confined to the Hyndburn area. Places such as Ripon, Caernarfon, Cannock Chase and Salisbury Plain do play a significant part. Above all, the Pals took part in the cataclysm that was the

Globe Centre.
(Hyndburn B.C)

1914-1918 war. From their beginnings in the industrial towns of east Lancashire they gladly served their country. They fought with honour and valour in the slaughter-house known as the Western Front. In common with other battalions of the East Lancashire Regiment, the Pals are now, to quote the Regimental motto, 'Known by their Deeds'. This book recounts a selection of the Pal's 'Deeds' and gives a guide to where they took place. It also gives a guide to where so many are buried and are commemorated. The book also follows a 'trail' in England and Wales to the places then and now associated with them.

Finally, the book follows the trail of two men, 15971 Pte. Fred Sayer of Burnley, and 24799 Pte. Percy Crabtree of Nelson. In 1938 they got together to write of their experiences in the war. The result was a typed, foolscap, manuscript, *The History of Z Company*. This is the source of the several personal accounts which follow.

Fred Sayer wrote the section from September 1914 to May 1917, Percy Crabtree from then to the Armistice (with an overlap from June 1916 to May 1917).

Both men's accounts, although very different in style, illustrate quite clearly how 'ordinary' men displayed extraordinary courage and devotion to duty in the vilest of situations. They did all this with the irrepressible humour and sang-froid so common to the 'squaddies' of the times.

N.B. For a more detailed story of the Pals read *Pals: The 11th (Service) Battalion (Accrington) East Lancashire Regiment*, published by Leo Cooper Pen and Sword Books, the book to which this *Accrington Pals Trail* is a companion volume.

Acknowledgements

My first acknowledgement, without doubt, must be to Percy Crabtree and Fred Sayer. My special thanks go to Percy's daughter, Mrs. Barbara Brown, and to Fred's daughter, Mrs. Judy Langton, for allowing me to use extracts from their fathers' material.

For more years than I care to remember I have been a member of Lancashire County Library and its various branches. I know more than most that any research of consequence can not be done without the professional help of public library staff, especially Local Studies and Reference Librarians. I am, therefore, extremely grateful for the help and advice of many librarians, in particular, Jean Siddal at Burnley, Mrs. E. Thomas at Caernarfon, Donald Brown at Cannock, Honor Tripp at Ripon and Bruce Purvis at Salisbury. Closer to home, Helen

Barrett, a Local Studies Librarian at Accrington, deserves a special mention for her keen interest in the Pals and her support. I thank her also for her article in Chapter Five.

I am also indebted to the staffs at the Tourist Information Centres in Accrington, Burnley, Chorley, Caernarfon, Cannock, Ripon and Salisbury for the help they gave me on my visits. In addition, Helene Heyes at Accrington has my special thanks for writing an article in Chapter Five.

Enid Briggs, the Revd. Dennis Crook and Peter Whelan, the playwright, were also kind enough to write articles for me. I offer them my grateful thanks.

I am also grateful to the curators and staffs of the various museums and record offices who so promptly answered my enquiries. I appreciate the help given by Chris Staerck of the Public Record Office at Kew. My thanks also to the P.R.O. for permission to use material they hold. The Commonwealth War Graves Commission at Maidenhead have, as always, been very helpful.

Many individuals have been helpful with their comments and advice and also with the loan of photographs and other material. These include Bob Ashton, Tony Bell, Bob and Pat Curley, John Fielding, Mr. Johnston, Barbara Kay, the late Gwen Kingsmill (for her kind permission to use John's photographs), Diccon Nelson-Roberts, Cllr. Ian Ormerod and staff of Hyndburn Council, Georges Rachaine, Larry Sagar, Wendy Saporita, Tony Spagnoly, Ken Turner, and Mr. C. J. Whitehouse. Their interest and willingness to help is very much appreciated.

I owe an enormous debt of gratitude to Peter Liddle, whose advice and encouragement has been invaluable. My thanks also go to him for so kindly writing the foreword and for his permission to use material from the Liddle Collection at the University of Leeds.

At the Pen and Sword offices I always get a friendly welcome – my thanks to Barbara Bramall and her staff. I am deeply grateful to Roni and Paul Wilkinson for their expertise and advice and to Charles Hewitt for his confidence in a 'Trail'.

My thanks go to Mike Clarke for putting my manuscript on disc, and in the process tidying up my typographical errors. And finally my thanks to Ruth for all her patience during my years of 'magnificent obsession'.

CHAPTER ONE

Private Fred Sayer's Story:
August 1914 -March 1916

1. Background Note on the Raising of the Battalion
2. Brief History of the Pals from September 1914 to March 1916,
*   told through the recollections of 15971 Pte. Fred Sayer*

1. Background Note on the Raising of the Battalion

Britain entered the war against Germany on 4 August 1914. Lord Kitchener, the Secretary of State for War, made his first appeal for 100,000 volunteers on 7 August. From that day his recruiting posters appeared on every hoarding and in every newspaper. Men in their thousands flocked to the newly opened recruiting stations in every town and city in the country.

On 19 August, in Liverpool, an appeal by Lord Derby resulted in the first of several 'Service' battalions of The King's (Liverpool Regiment). The idea of citizens of the same town, recruited, equipped and serving together, greatly appealed to many. Lord Derby's initiative excited the imagination of Lord Mayors and municipalities all over the country. Patriotism and civic pride, and the opportunity to serve with

(Accrington Observer and Times)

WHAT IS YOUR ANSWER TO YOUR COUNTRY'S CALL?

JOIN THE ACCRINGTON & DISTRICT "PALS" BATTALION.

This Cartoon will be shown on the screens of the Picture Houses in Accrington & District.

friends and neighbours, inspired many thousands of men to enlist in the 'Pals' battalions of Lord Kitchener's New Army.

On 6 September, the Mayor of Accrington, Councillor John Harwood, decided to raise his own battalion. Recruitment started in Accrington and the surrounding townships of Clayton-le-Moors, Church, Great Harwood, Oswaldtwistle and Rishton, plus the neighbouring boroughs of Blackburn, Burnley and Chorley. Over a thousand men enlisted in ten days. Thirty-six officers were appointed.

The Mayor with the officers of the Battalion, February, 1915.
Top row (left to right): **Lt J Ramsbottom; 2/Lt G G Williams; 2/Lt W Slinger; 2/Lt C D Haywood; 2/Lt H Ashworth; Lt C W Gidlow-Jackson; 2/Lt F Bailey; 2/Lt W R Roberts.** *Second row* (left to right): **Mr W J Newton (Accrington Borough Surveyor): 2/Lt C Stonehouse; 2/Lt T W Rawcliffe; 2/Lt J V Kershaw; 2/Lt A B Tough; 2/Lt H H Mitchell; 2/Lt J C Shorrocks; 2/Lt E Jones; 2/Lt W G M Rigby.** *Third row* (left to right): **Lt Campbell (RAMC); 2/Lt F A Heys; 2/Lt L Ryden; 2/Lt F G MacAlpine; 2/Lt F Birtwistle; Lt T J Kenny; 2/Lt T Y Harwood; 2/Lt M E Whittaker; 2/Lt J H Ruttle; Lt H D Riley.** *Front row* (left to right): **Hon Capt and Quartermaster G Lay: Capt W H Cheney; Capt H Livesey; Capt R Ross; Major G N Slinger; The Mayor, John Harwood, J P; Col R Sharples; Capt J C Milton; Capt P J Broadley; Capt A G Watson; Lt A Peltzer.**

The Accrington 'Pals' came into being. The 11th. (Service) Battalion (Accrington) of the East Lancashire Regiment was but one of what was to become some four hundred Service Battalions of Kitchener's New Army.

In the Accrington Pals were four Companies of approximately 250 men each: 'Accrington' (A), 'The Districts' (B), 'Chorley' (C) and 'Burnley' (D). The Chorley and Burnley Companies were formed, and trained initially, in their home towns. The Accrington Pals had the distinction of being, firstly, the only battalion raised by a non-county borough, and secondly, the only one with the name of a town as part of its official title.

(Local Studies Library, Accrington.)

— G. R. —

Accrington 'Pals' Batt.

(11th Service Batt. E.L. Regt.)

War Office has sent orders for the 6th Depot Company (Reserve) of

250 Men To Be Raised At Once.

It is hoped that Accrington and Burnley boys will fill up the ranks as soon as possible.

Recruits accepted at any Recruiting Office.

Height from 5ft. 1in. and Chest measurement from 34in.

Full Army Allowances, including Separation Allowances to families.

Khaki Uniforms and full Kits provided on joining Reserve Companies at Chadderton Camp.

RALLY ROUND THE FLAG.

GOD SAVE THE KING.

Fred Sayer was born in Burnley in 1897. After the war he qualified as an Insurance Surveyor, at which profession he worked throughout the north of England. In 1940, in Morecambe, he helped form the 4th. (South Lonsdale) Home Guard. He retired as Lt. Colonel in 1945. He was a well-known north Lancashire hotelier, a respected authority on fishing and a talented potter. He retired in 1962. He was married with a daughter and a son. He died at his home in Nottingham, aged 91, on 9 January 1989.

2. Brief history of the Pals from September 1914 to March 1916, told through the recollections of 15971 Pte. Fred Sayer

In 1912 fourteen year old Fred Sayer was sacked by a Burnley printer for running the printing machines too fast.

'My energetic nature began to get the better of me and I got into the habit of speeding the machines up when doing small stuff. The faster they went the more the floor shook and workers down below complained. The owner sent for my father and said, "For Gott's sake take him away!". (I think he was a German).'

Fred's father, a clerk at a local manufacturing chemist, got him a job as a helper to Dr. Hodges, a General Practitioner in Burnley.

'My initiation into the medical world was sudden and severe. Dr. Hodges showed me the dispensary wherein I was to work. It was a long, narrow, room with a coal fire burning merrily. There was a massive iron kettle, always on the boil. Six wooden chairs were tucked under a table. There were bottles of Lysol [a disinfectant] and enamel bowls. There was a bench and a cabinet for dangerous drugs. Bottles of other drugs, boxes of ointment and powders occupied shelves which covered every spare inch of the walls. Dr. Hodges took a bowl, splashed in some Lysol and filled the bowl with boiling water, tempered it with some cold from the tap, and shouted.'

'In response, a miner walked in, took a chair, stripped a bandage from his hand and popped his hand into the bowl. After a few minutes of soaking Dr. Hodges showed me a most ghastly mess and renewed the dressing very quickly. As the man walked away, Dr. Hodges looked me in the eye and

16

Men and Boys at a Burnley Pit in 1912. Note the 'bait tin' and the short handled picks for use in the narrow seams. *(Local Studies Library, Burnley)*

said "You can manage that". I was paralysed but managed to nod my head. He then left to attend his surgery in the next room and a queue of miners exploded into the room to fill all the empty chairs. With their co-operation I renewed their dressings. They were a rough lot, poor, kindly and tough, and although they knew I was a novice they treated me in an encouraging way and at the end of the day I felt I had justified my existence. The sheer pressure of work was an admirable teacher and I enjoyed learning the skills required.'

Fred wasn't to know that these skills – and others – learnt at Dr. Hodges' were to stand him in good stead.

In September 1914 Mr. Raymond Ross, Burnley Borough Analyst, and a former cavalry officer, became Officer Commanding, Burnley Company of the Accrington Pals. At that time, part of seventeen year old Fred Sayer's duties was to take samples of blood and sputum to Ross's department in the Town Hall for testing. This contact led to Fred's enlistment in the Pals.

'I knew Mr. Ross would tell Dr. Hodges I had joined up, so that evening after surgery I plucked up courage and told him in a casual sort of way. He just looked up and said I was a bloody fool for joining the infantry when I could have waited a few months and gone into the RAMC. He was annoyed, mostly because he would be inconvenienced. I said that, if he wished, I

Manchester Road, Burnley, from St James' Street circa 1914. The Town Hall (Clock Tower) is on the right. *(Local Studies Library, Burnley).*

could carry on with morning and evening surgeries as our parade didn't start until 10 am and I was free Saturday and Sundays. He liked this, so I still got my ten shillings a week, plus billeting allowance, plus sixpence a day, so I became top earner in our household. For several weeks I played this double role, then fortunately for my health, parades started at 8.30 am and we had evening and weekend training sessions. So it was good-bye to the medical world, my prospects, and the slavery of a twelve hour day.'

Mr. now Captain, Ross, as Company Commander, was required with his officers, to 'live in' at the Territorial Drill Hall in Burnley which served as Company H.Q. Fred was given the job of purchasing the Officers Mess food and drink from the local shops and assisting the caretaker's wife with the cooking and cleaning. 'Don't forget, Sayer', said Captain Ross, 'when you are in Burnley on Company business, you represent the Company'. Each morning Fred attended early parade, then went into Burnley town centre to order food and wine, etc.

for delivery, all paid for by the Mess. Usually, the heaviest thing he carried was a box of cigars or cigarettes. He also, with two batmen, 'lived in'. For this he got an extra one pound a week. It was the 'cushiest' of 'cushy' jobs .

He also got other jobs to do. One of the Company had not been on parade for over a week.

'Captain Ross called me into his office and showed me a brief note – 'Cannot come on parade, bowels bad'. "Ah! Sayer, we'll teach him a lesson. I want you to take two men, with rifle and bayonet, and an enema. When you knock on his door have a man either side of you. Show him the enema and describe it's purpose. Any water you need you'll get there, but I don't think you will need it". That evening we duly presented ourselves at the house. A poor little thing answered the door and got the fright of her life. Keeping a straight face I asked to be shown the sick man. As we suspected, he was down the pub, but she wouldn't say which one. We decided to leave the matter in her capable hands and before we reported the next morning the man was already on parade. He wasn't punished apart from a 'ticking off' but he was the object of ridicule when the story got out.'

In February 1915 the Pals left their respective home towns of Accrington, Burnley and Chorley and entrained for Caernarvon (now Caernarfon, Gwynedd), north Wales. Fred lost his job and the pound a week and became batman to Lt. J. V. Kershaw, who, with the rest of the officers, now lived at the Royal Hotel. On March 1st. the Battalion was taken over by Lt. Col. A. W. Rickman of the Northumberland Fusiliers. He was a truly professional soldier and quickly smartened up the Battalion. Amongst other administrative changes he redesignated the four companies. 'A' (Accrington) became 'W' Company; B' (Districts) 'X'; 'C' (Chorley) 'Y' and 'D' (Burnley) became 'Z' Company.

During the Battalion's three months stay at

Lt. Col. A W Rickman of the Northumberland Fusiliers took formal command of the 11th East Lancashire Regiment at Caernarvon on 1 March 1915. This photograph was taken in London in 1918. Lt. Col. Rickman died aged 51 in a tragic accident involving an electricity generator at his home 16 October 1925. *(The Pals Collection)*

Don't be Alarmed,
the Accrington Pals are
on guard at Carnarvon.

(The Pals Collection)

Caernarvon more equipment and uniforms arrived and the 'toughening-up' routines were beginning to take effect. Fred Sayer again escaped most of the parade-ground disciplines.

'In becoming a gentleman's personal servant from being the "Company's representative" I had stepped down in the social scale somewhat. I wondered if I had been wise taking the job but I quickly realised it was not just the extra sixpence a day I was getting but the freedom of missing parades which was the real reward. Furthermore, a good cup of tea in the early morning had become important to me. Bill (Lt. Frank Heys' batman) dreaded making early morning tea as officers were fussy in their little demands. No one, however, could clean and polish like Bill so we came to an amicable arrangement. All I had to do was make the teas, tidy up both officers dressing-tables, etc., and take both lots of washing to the laundry. As I took my own, this was no chore at all.'

On 13 May 1915 the Battalion left Caernarvon for Rugeley Camp, Staffordshire. There they joined with the 12th (Service) York and Lancaster Regiment (Sheffield City), the 13th (Service) York and Lancaster Regiment (1st Barnsley), and the 14th (Service) York and Lancaster Regiment (2nd Barnsley) to become 94 Brigade, 31st Division. (The four battalions were to continue their close relationship until February 1918).

Battalion and Brigade training was carried out on the moorland near the camp during the glorious weather of May, June and July. The Battalion was slowly taking shape as an effective unit. Specialist groups such as signallers, machine-gunners, bandsmen/stretcher-bearers, clerical and transport staff were formed with either volunteers or 'pressed men'. Meanwhile Fred and his friend Bill continued as batmen to their two lieutenants. Life became a lot tougher. The perks

20

A group of 'Z' Company men at Rugeley Camp, Pte Fred Sayer is pictured centre (circled). *(Mrs J Langton)*

of comfortable billets and home comforts were gone to be replaced by a wooden hut shared with twenty-eight others, with ablutions in the open air. This time batmen were not excused any training.

> *'We started early and finished late, our free time was spent putting out moorland fires which continually threatened some part of the vast camp. It was hard but healthy work.'*

On 30 July the Battalion left Rugeley for a recruiting visit to the home towns of Accrington, Blackburn, Burnley and Chorley. All went on a welcome leave. After four days they entrained for Ripon, north Yorkshire. Ripon was now transformed from a quiet market town to a vast military camp with some 30,000 troops in the area.

Everyone in the Battalion, from officers, N.C.O.'s, cooks, sanitary men, batmen, et al, completed his musketry course. The complete firing course, on ranges with targets at one hundred yards to six hundred yards, took four weeks. After being in the army for eleven months it was the first time most had fired a shot.

Even at Ripon Fred continued his penchant for having more than one job at a time, each being in his words – 'Cushy'. One day he and another man, Bob, [like Bill we never know his surname] were temporarily relieved of all training obligations in and out of camp, given a new uniform and a bicycle and told to report to Ripley Castle, near Harrogate, the residence of Brigadier General Carter-Campbell, 94 Brigade Commander, to work as runners.

On 2 August 1915 the Battalion returned to Accrington from Rugeley Camp en-route to Ripon. Here, in the town centre, they are about to be dismissed for four days leave. *(The Pals collection)*

'We both set off, we said not a word. We were suffering from shock and neither of us wanted it. I had a nice job, I was a batman with only tea to make. I got 3/6d less a shilling for Bill.

The scene in 1998. *(The Author)*

I wondered if I could manage both jobs. The new job turned out better than we ever expected. We lived in the coach-house at the rear, a dry, clean place. Here one or the other of us must be on duty from 0800 hours to 1800 hours each day. Our duties were to take messages by bicycle to anywhere as ordered by the Corps Commander or his staff. A staff Captain inspected our bicycles, thought they were heavy-weights, and gave us a chit to purchase a lighter one at the shop in Ripon. If I had any complaints, I must contact him. Complaints indeed! Was I dreaming? We could arrange our duty schedule amongst ourselves and so give each other every other day off! We asked a clerk what else we were expected to do. He said, 'Get a good book, sit in one of the deck-chairs and enjoy yourselves!' My only job on the first day was to do some shopping in Ripon for the house-keeper. It was bliss! Sheer bliss!'

(The Pals Collection)

Fred's concern about losing his batman's job was needless. He quickly made arrangements with Bill and Lts. Kershaw and Heys and then easily settled into his dual role of batman and runner.

'Ripon, Harrogate, Bolton Abbey, the Dales and the Yorkshire moors were a happy reward for my adventurous soul. With my Corps pass I could come and go without interference. I visited my Aunt at Aysgarth and came back loaded with food for the boys in camp including once a cooked chicken.'

Fred was a shrewd young man however, and he knew this sort of life could not go on forever and, indeed, was not why he enlisted. Early in September 1915 he volunteered to be a member of 'Z' Company's sixteen strong 'Bombers' – specialists in hand-grenades. The training for this was in addition to normal duties, so for a short time Fred had three jobs – batman, runner and bomber. On 24 September the Battalion moved south to Salisbury Plain. Fred and Bob declined the opportunity of staying with Corps H.Q. Fred also decided that when the time came to go abroad he would finish being a batman. He saw his future as a bomber and nothing else. He enjoyed the company of his fellow-bombers and he was , in his own words, "Fighting fit and ready for anything".

Divisional training started on Salisbury Plain. The weather turned foul. 'Salisbury Plain was big enough for battleships and sometimes wet enough for submarines.' The specialists continued their training – and the 'Burly Bombers' of 'Z' Company had exciting times.

'Our job was to train for 'dangerous enterprises against the enemy', learn the use of gun-cotton, fuses and detonators, how to make and throw bombs made from jam tins and how to fire rifle-grenades. Quite often we had an early breakfast and armed with gun-cotton etc., and spades and bread and cheese for a mid-day meal, we marched miles to find the filthiest field of clay. We then dug a trench so we were knee deep in mud and only then would our instructor allow us to indulge ourselves. Sweat (or was it rain?) streamed from us as we flung our little charges and watched out for little wisps of smoke as they exploded.'

By early December 1915 it was the view of many Pals that it was about time the Battalion went on active service. Their wishes were realised when the Battalion was warned to leave camp for an unknown destination. It was not however, to be France as most expected. 'Rumour had it as 'somewhere in the East', the Cookhouse said 'Gallipoli', Watercart said 'India'. On 22 December 31st Division received orders to embark for Egypt on 6 December, 94 Brigade to embark between 18 and 28 of December.

A group of 'Z' Company men at Hurdcott Camp, December 1915. Pte John Murphy (Killed in Action 1 July 1916) is circled. *(Miss Ann Lister)*

What 'Cookhouse' and 'Watercart' and others did not know was that by the autumn of 1915 the British High Command had recognised the Allied campaign at Gallipoli in the Dardenelles had failed. The assaults at Anzac Cove and Cape Helles in April 1915 and a further landing at Suvla Bay in August had proved arduous and costly in men's lives and left the Turkish defences as impregnable as ever. In October the decision was made to evacuate. On 18 December. British and Anzac troops left Suvla Bay. On 8 January. 1916 the last troops safely left Cape Helles and Gallipoli was left to the Turks.

(Amongst these last troops were the 4th. (Blackburn) and the 5th. (Burnley) Battalions of the East Lancashire Regiment (Territorial Force), amongst whom many of the Pals had friends or relatives).

Pte E Shuttleworth (centre) poses with two friends in a Salisbury studio shortly before leaving for Egypt. *(The Pals Collection)*

The British High Command feared an attack on Egypt by the Turkish forces now released from Gallipoli. 31st Division, originally destined for France, was diverted to Egypt to be part of the Imperial Strategic Reserve defending the Suez Canal. On Wednesday 15 December the 11th. East Lancashire Regiment, as part of 94 Brigade, 31st Division, received orders to embark at Devonport on 19 December. The Battalion made its final march in England in the early Sunday morning hours along the empty roads and sleeping streets of Salisbury. No band, no singing, no shouted commands, just the steady tramp of boots as they marched to the railway station, en-route for Devonport. At five p.m. the same day the TSS *Ionic* moved off on her voyage to Egypt to the sound of 'Auld Lang Syne' played by a band on the quayside.

Fred Sayer was no longer a batman and he settled down to enjoy the voyage. He missed the extra 3/6 a week and the extra cups of tea and he found he missed the relative independence and privacy he had had as a batman. Two or three days out at sea however, he was on deck enjoying the sea air when he found Lt. Kershaw at his side.

'Lt. Kershaw hinted that he missed my cheerful presence and my successor was willing and tidy but couldn't really make a good cup of tea. Just what the doctor ordered, thought I! "Shall I give him a few days training for free? I'd enjoy something to do" Kershaw beamed. "Help yourself, Sayer." So I finished up in the quiet and comfort of the officers quarters, if only on a part-time basis, for a few days. Life was a little more pleasant, I could even have a shower when the tenants were otherwise engaged.'

Fred and his fellow-bombers were kept busy at other times, however. There were daily sessions of 'Swedish Drill' and weapons training classes and lectures were held every morning. The afternoons were given to sports and games. Boxing, wrestling, pillow fights on a spar and so on were all enjoyed. The efforts were always good-humoured.

'The prize of the day went to one of the Ionic's *officers. Our tug-of-war team, mostly made up of us bombers, was practising by pulling on a rope attached to a bollard. Sergeant Wilson was shouting "Heave! Heave!" when a stern looking gold-braided, cap-wearing officer suddenly yelled at him "Stop! You fool, you'll have the bloody boat over!" Operations ceased, the officer went on his way, the rope was taken off the bollard. Then the penny dropped. We'd been had, and at our roar of laughter the officer grinned at us. Unfortunately, Sgt. Wilson was the last to get the joke and he thought we were laughing at him.'*

Sadly, the Battalion's first death on active service occurred on the voyage. Pte. James Wixted 15835, of Accrington, died of Siriasis (sunstroke) on 29 December. He was buried at sea south-west of Crete at 6 a.m., 30 December. His name is commemorated on the Helles Memorial, Gallipoli.

After a relatively uneventful journey, although some would disagree when on New Years Eve a German submarine fired a torpedo at the ship – and missed – the *Ionic* arrived at Alexandria on 1 January. 1916[1]. The Battalion finally disembarked at Port Said on 5 January. On the 25 January they moved to El Ferdan on the banks of the Suez Canal. Here their duties included operating a chain driven flat-bottomed ferry, usually filled with men, horses and stores, across the Canal. Teams of sixteen men each hauled on two chains which lay on the canal bed. The 'Burly Bombers' were ideal for this task.

'All day long we loaded or unloaded in turn stacks of food, stores, wagons, horses, mules, bales of hay etc., with all kinds of people in between. We were worn out by noon, but were driven

The landing stage at Port Said, where the *Ionic* disembarked in January 1916. *(The Pals Collection)*

on and on. We were rusty, dusty and musty and we must have been a bit smelly too. We got though, a few laughs to help us along. The first came when it was Sgt. Wilson's turn to be with us. As he shouted "Heave, you lot. Heave! Come on!" someone shouted, "Stop! You'll have the bloody boat over!" The slave-driver was furious! Funny how some sergeants had no sense of humour. The next joke was on me. There I was, half-dead, my hands red raw, and there, sitting on a box watching the performance, was Lt. Kershaw's batman. As I looked at him, sweat filled my eyes and I had to wipe them with my sleeve. He didn't say anything, but he looked sympathetic.'

By mid-February it became clear that the Turks were unlikely to risk an attack on the Suez Canal across the Sinai Desert. The British High Command, therefore, decided that by April 1916 (the beginning of the dry season) three divisions could defend the Canal instead of the present twelve. This meant that more troops could be spared for what was always considered the more important theatre of war in France and Belgium.

As early as 6 December 1915, at the second Allied Military Conference at Chantilly, held to discuss Allied operations for the coming year, Great Britain and France, in a joint enterprise with Russia and Italy, decided to deliver simultaneous attacks with maximum forces on their respective fronts, 'as soon as circumstances were favourable', probably in the Spring of 1916. By February 1916 this changed to June or July for a joint British and French attack astride the River Somme where both armies met.

After the Chantilly Conference the British High Command readied their full strength in men and material in preparation for the great offensive, with the ruling principle to place every possible division, fully equipped, in France by Spring. This released several divisions in the Imperial Strategic Reserve, amongst them 31st Division, for France and the 'Big Push'. 46th Division was the first to leave and sailed from Egypt on 4 February 1916. On 26 February. 31st Division received orders to embark for France. Three days later the 11th. East Lancashire Regiment got just two days notice to leave Port Said on 2 March. The Battalion marched into Port Said docks and immediately boarded the TSS *Llandovery Castle*. She sailed as soon as all were aboard.

The Battalion left behind two men. Lt. Henry Mitchell of Hoghton, near Blackburn, was seriously injured on 21 February, in an accident on the light railway at El Kantara. He died two days later. He was buried in Port Said War Memorial Cemetery, grave no. J21. Pte. William Baron 15478 of Rishton was left in hospital seriously ill. He died on March 23rd. and is buried nearby in grave no. J7.

The six-day voyage to Marseilles was comfortable and uneventful. At 9 a.m. on 9 March, two hours after disembarking, the Battalion entrained for the Front. The train was old, with wooden seats and no glass in the windows. The men were packed in tightly. The rickety train travelled as best it could across France until, at last, at 11 a.m. on 11 March, 1916, just fifty hours after leaving Marseilles, came the end of the line at Pont Remy, on the River Somme, near Abbeville.

The train journey had been miserable and wearisome and when Pont Remy was reached there was a concerted sigh of relief. This lessened somewhat in the bitterly cold March wind. The Battalion, still incongruously wearing pith helmets, marched six miles to their billets of barns, outhouses and cottages in the village of Huppy, south of Pont Remy. Everyone felt good and thankful to be marching along a solid highway once again.

In Huppy those unfortunates of 'Z' Company placed in barns complained to Major Ross about the flea-ridden straw and the rats scuttling about. His reply came, 'You're in France now my lads, so you'd better get used to it'.

1. In January 1920, in the House of Commons, Mr. Dan Irving, M.P. for Burnley, reminded the Secretary of State for War, Mr. Winston Churchill, that the Battalion had, in 1918, been refused the 1914-15 Star because 'it was not engaged with the enemy in 1915' and asked him to reconsider the matter. Winston Churchill replied that because the Battalion had not disembarked in a theatre of war during 1915 they were not eligible under the conditions governing the award of the Star and no exceptions could be made. Most of the men were convinced that having a torpedo fired at them was 'being engaged with the enemy', New Year's Eve or not. Even eighty years after the event, surviving veterans were still convinced they were wrongly denied their 'rightful' 1914-15 Star.

CHAPTER TWO

The Somme:
March 1916 - December 1916

1. Accidental Deaths in the Line
Pte. Fred Sayer:

> '*On 27 May an incident of immense distress concerned one of our original Pals. On a bright summer morning with a certain amount of peace about in the front line, this quiet, steady soldier was cleaning his rifle. It was a drill and he must have done it a thousand times or more. As he finished, he snapped the bolt in place and pulled the trigger. Being in the front line he did not point the rifle skywards, as was usual, for safety's sake.*'

> '*He did not know how it happened but a bullet went through his two pals, killing them both instantly. The anguish of this poor soul can be imagined to some degree, but I cannot conceive anyone realising the suffering he experienced. He was inconsolable. He volunteered for all the dangerous jobs and we knew he was looking for something "with his name on it". He was killed on 1 July, in company with many of his pals, which was what he wanted.*'

Mystery surrounds this incident. Pte. Sayer's story was corroborated to the author, quite independently, by a veteran present at the time. He described how he, and others, were amazed that the bullet entered the body of the first man at one angle and came out at another – presumably deflected by bone or muscle. The bullet hit the second man, who was seated at the time, in the chest.

The veteran added that although the incident was common knowledge throughout the battalion, no action was taken. Indeed, the

29

words 'hushed up' were used. The reason for this is a matter of conjecture but possibly senior officers were anxious to continue with the intense preparations for the forthcoming attack.

The Battalion War Diary offers no clue. The entries for the relevant period simply state:

20 May – Battalion to front line and occupied K29c 1535 to K23d 2535 (map references).

25 May – For first five days no casualties. All available men were working on improvement of front line trench and wiring par ties out every night.

27 May – Two killed, eight wounded.

29 May – Seven wounded. Total casualties in this tour of the trenches – 2 killed, 23 wounded.

30 May – Battalion relieved by 14 York and Lancaster Regiment – to Brigade reserve, Courcelles.

The following letter was written by 'W' Company Commander, Capt. R. B. Tough, to Miss M. Jackson of Clayton-le-Moors:-

Pte T Jackson. *(Mr Eric Shaw)*

'It is with deepest regret that I have to inform you that your brother, Pte. T. Jackson, was killed in action yesterday, May 27th. He was a splendid soldier and a very bright and cheerful comrade and I can assure you that his death has cast a gloom over the whole company, with whom he was very popular. He was shot through the chest and died practically instantaneously and suffered no pain. I would like, on behalf of the officers and men of his company to express to you our deepest sympathy. – Capt. R. B. Tough.'

Sucrerie Military Cemetery, Colincamps.
(The Pals Collection)

An identical letter was received by the widow of Pte. Robert Pickering of Darwen. Something about the tone of this letter led Miss Jackson to believe this was not the truth. Her enquiries brought no result, and her suspicions were only confirmed when a comrade came home on leave. The name of the soldier responsible was never revealed.

Pte. Thomas Jackson 15935 of Clayton-le-Moors and Pte. Robert Pickering 15942 of Darwen, are buried in Sucrerie Military Cemetery, Colicamps, Grave numbers 1H 53 and 54 respectively.

2. Pte Percy Crabtree – June

On 24 June 1916, a week before the attack on Serre, the Battalion received at Louvencourt a final draft of fifty-eight other ranks and one officer from 12 (Reserve) Battalion at Prees Heath, Shropshire. Amongst them was 24799 Pte. Percy Crabtree, age 28.

Pte. Crabtree enlisted in Nelson in March 1916. He spent ten weeks in training before coming to France. After a short stay at Etaples, he and the rest of the draft arrived at Louvencourt. They had missed the Battalion rehearsals for the attack held at Gezaincourt in mid-June so there was time only for the briefest of preparation and training before 1 July.

Percy, in later years, never spoke of his experiences on that day. We do know that he, in common with the rest of the draft, went into the trenches for the first time ever on 30 June. We also know that two friends, 24787 Pte. Thomas Taylor, age 29, and 24797 Pte. James Allan Watson, age 28, were killed in action. Another friend, 24798 Pte. W. Mallinson, was wounded.

Pte. Taylor is commemorated on the Thiepval Memorial, whilst Pte. Watson is buried in Euston Road Cemetery in grave no. I G 22.

Percy Crabtree was born in Padiham, near Burnley, in 1888. He returned to teaching after the war. After several local posts he became headmaster of Lomeshaye School, Nelson. In 1944 he was appointed headmaster of Bradley School, Nelson. He retired in 1948. He had a strong religious faith, working all his life for the Methodist church. He was a life-long teetotaller. He was an enthusiastic local historian, photographer and artist in water-colour. He was married with one daughter. He died at his home in Nelson on 8 November 1958.

(Mrs B Brown)

31

4. 1st July, 1916

The story of 1 July need not be told in any detail. The following brief outline is sufficient. Further information can be obtained from *Pals, The 11th (Service) Battalion (Accrington) East Lancashire Regiment*, published by Pen & Sword Books Ltd.

The Western Front
Approximate line 1916

By the end of June some fifteen divisions of General Sir H. Rawlinson's fourth Army were in readiness for the 'Big Push' on 1 July. In Lt. Gen. Sir A. G. Hunter-Weston's VIII Corps were four divisions of which one was 31st Division. 31st Division was made up of three Brigades – 92, 93 and 94. The Pals in company with the Sheffield City Battalion and the two Barnsley battalions of the York and Lancaster Regiment, made up 94 Brigade.

The principle objective of the British troops in the 'Push' was to break through the German defences on an eighteen-mile front from Gommecourt in the north, to Maricourt on the River Somme in the south, and continue eastwards and northwards into the open country beyond. The main task of 31st Division was to capture the fortified village of Serre and secure the northern flank of the hoped-for main breakthrough further south.

The Pals and the City Battalion were to make the initial assault on Serre on 1 July, with the two Barnsley battalions following through. On 24 June there began a bombardment from over 1,400 British guns 'softening up', or so it was hoped, the German defences in readiness for the assault.

At 7.30 a.m. in the bright sunshine of 1 July over 700 Pals advanced from their trenches before Serre. Seven days of British artillery fire was supposed to have obliterated the German positions. As the Pals came slowly across the three hundred yards of No Man's Land the

A farm house in Serre before 1 July 1916. Note the German soldier near the gateway. (Arrowed) *(Mr John Bailey)*

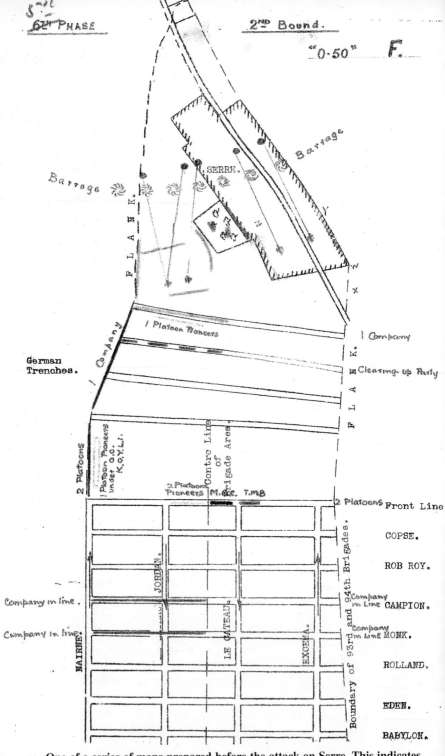

One of a series of maps prepared before the attack on Serre. This indicates the expected positions of each company in the second bound. *(WO95/2341 PRO)*

German defenders came up from deep dugouts untouched by the shelling and swept the advancing troops with machine-gun and rifle fire. A few got into the German trenches, a few reached Serre itself but these were never seen or heard of again. Most of the Pals lay in heaps before the barbed wire defences. In less than twenty minutes some 235 Pals died and 350 lay wounded. The attack on Serre was completely repulsed.

1 July is so important, however, that it can not be described without the addition of some sort of personal account.

2/Lt (later Captain) Bart Endean.
(Mr Tony Bell)

The following tell their own story. Firstly, 2/Lt. Bartholomew (Bart) Endean (before the attack), secondly Pte. Fred Sayer (during the attack) and thirdly, Pte. Harry Fielding's account, in a letter home, of his capture (one of very few that day). Pte. Sayer ends the selection with a description of his return to the rear after the failure of the attack.

a) 2/Lt. Bart Endean, posted to 'Z' Company in April 1916, and later to be the Company Commander, had an experience which possibly saved his life:

'The night before 1 July we set off from camp and got into the trenches, maybe at 3 o'clock in the morning. Everyone was carrying extra stuff – extra rations, extra ammunition, flares, flags and all sorts of things. You could hardly move in the trench.'

'After we had got everybody fixed up I said to Sgt. Ingham "Let's have a cup of Oxo in that dug-out" The two of us went down, boiled some water on a methylated spirit stove and had a drink of Oxo. When we were coming up again, I thought I would take my equipment off so that I'd be able to move about more easily in the trench. I took it off and hung it on a nail at the bottom of the dug-out steps.

'We were due to go over the top at half-past seven. At seven o'clock it was, a beautiful morning and the sun was already shining. I made my way to the dug-out, thinking that I'd better get my equipment on. I was just going down the steps when Sgt. Ingham said, "I'll give you a hand, Sir". He followed me down. I took my equipment off the nail, turned around, gave it to him, turned around again and I was putting my arms out for him to put the straps over, when a shell dropped right on top of the dug-out.

Captain 'Jack' Roberts.
(Mr Diccon Nelson-Roberts)

'When I came to, I said to myself, 'There goes all my bloody teeth!''. But it wasn't my teeth. It was a mouthful of dirt I was spitting out. I couldn't see. I couldn't get up – every time I tried there was something lying across my back – I think it must have been the timber of the dug-out. I remember saying to myself "I wonder if I've got a Blighty one?". I couldn't tell whether I was bleeding. I couldn't feel anything the matter with me. And I didn't know where the sergeant was.

'After a while I could see a streak of sunlight coming from a corner – one streak of light coming through the darkness as if it were coming from a keyhole. I thought that if I could get nearer to it I might make the hole a bit bigger. But I couldn't get up. I tried again. I pressed downwards to try to get up and the Sergeant groaned. I knew then he was underneath me. I couldn't see him. I heard someone shout – "Can you get out here, Sir?". The fellows had got on the top from the trench and had lifted the sandbags and the battens off. I was able to get down into the trench.

'I went to look for the company commander, Captain Riley. Someone must have told him what had happened because he was coming towards me. He put his arm around my shoulder and said "My God, Endean, what's happened?". I told him, "Sergeant Ingham's in the dug-out – will you get him out?". He sent me straight to the Medical Officer [Captain 'Jack' Roberts RAMC] at the Regimental Aid Post (in Railway Hollow). I remember thinking that I would kid the M.O. into giving me a drop of rum, but all I got was "Rum? You can't have any rum, but here's a tetanus injection!.

'I wasn't badly hurt. Just bits of shrapnel. After about four nights in hospital in France, I came to England. When I eventually got back to the Battalion I found that Sergeant Ingham had died from his wounds. If he hadn't said "I'll give you a hand, Sir", he would have been here now."'

Sgt. Ben Ingham 15368 of Burnley, is buried in Euston Road Cemetery, Colincamps, Grave number I D 9.

b) Pte. Fred Sayer, sick and excused duties, volunteered to look after Z Company's reserve bomb store. With two others he was in a dug-out ready to issue bombs when required. Nobody came. His two

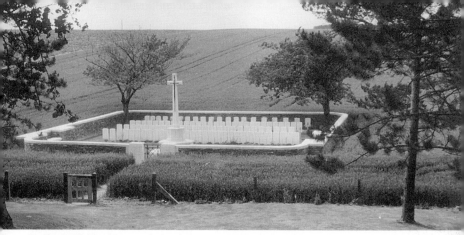

Railway Hollow cemetery from the rear of the trench line. *(The Pals Collection)*

colleagues left the dug-out and Pte. Sayer was alone:

> '*I had on a new wrist-watch, which I had received for my birthday in four days time. It was only a cheap 'Ingersoll' but it was my only contact with my family at that moment. Then I was aware that someone had joined me. He was one of the Brigade's Cycle Company's men. He said they were in the attack. He had not been in the trenches before and asked what he should do. He had come too far forward and had strayed from his unit. He was badly shocked at having this terrifying experience. I suggested that if he saw his company going past at Zero, he could join them, but he had better get down and wait or he wouldn't join anything.*

> '*Suddenly there appeared hundreds of men coming past us. I looked at my watch. It was Zero. The men were coming over as if on parade, with bayonets fixed, but with rifles carried at the trail.*

> '*It was uncanny and unbelievable where everybody went. The German barrage was heavy and deadly and machine-gun fire from the flanks and front covered every inch of ground, killing and pinning down the entire attack almost before it had begun. Many shells were dropping and I flung myself down near the cyclist. Then, I was conscious of recovering from something. I had a lovely experience. I had ascended weightless into space with all the colours of the rainbow all around. I did not want to come back to earth. I could not hear anything, but there was an awful smell and my head was hot. I took off my steel helmet and a steel splinter which had penetrated the metal was burning the thick wool felt. I knocked it out and quickly put the helmet back on . I said something to the cyclist but he did not reply. I felt*

37

giddy and light-headed. How long I had been unconscious I had no idea. My mouth was dry, my eyes and nose were bunged up with gas-tainted earth, but it was not until I reached for my water-bottle that I realised that something was badly wrong. I was full of blood and gore. I looked at my limbs, felt at myself all over, but all seemed there. The cyclist was there too, buried to the waist and looking to his front, as before.

'Some of the water quenched my thirst and some helped to clean up a little. Then I realised that the bombs in the dump would not be required and I had wasted my endeavours. I was very tired. I was dazed, but I knew where I was and what I was detailed to do. I examined myself again and seemed o.k., but the bayonet on my rifle was broken off and the bolt had snapped although it fitted in metal grooves. As time passed our barrage seemed to weaken into nothing, but the Germans gave no respite and their heavies pounded the forward areas as well as the rear, where they probably thought our reserves would be forming.

'Reasonable thought came and went. I dozed but did not sleep. Suddenly, in the late afternoon, for the first time that day, I was afraid. I realised, for the first time, I had been concussed. With the return to consciousness, I recovered the will to survive. But I was still weightless as if I was intoxicated. However, only then did I realise that since Zero hour I had been talking to the dead. Crawling the few yards which separated us, I examined my silent comrade. The poor lad had been killed by the same shell that concussed me. From the waist down there was nothing. His lower half appeared to be buried, but in reality he was upright on his stump. He was still looking towards the enemy, with his helmet at a rakish angle. His face was white but not care-worn and he had no blemish on any visible part. If he had a similar experience to my heavenly flight, I thought, he must have had a lovely death.

'I now realised where the mess I'd been cleaning from my equipment came from. There was nothing I could do, except leave the cyclist as my silent companion. I'm sure he died painlessly. I remembered him being lost, it seemed a long time ago. He was very afraid and I was very sorry for him. It was a terrible crime to send people like him into battle without preparation or training. I was angry for him, not because of the war, or that I was in my present predicament, but because he should not have been there.'

c) Pte. Harry Fielding – prisoner of war

Pte. H. Fielding 24137
X Company, 11th E.L.R.
Kriegsgefangenen Stammlager, Nurnberg,
Bayern, Germany.

Dear Aunty,

I hope that you received the post-card which I sent a week ago. I am doing nicely at present, my leg I think will soon be quite right and the doctor says my face is doing well. Of course it is very painful, especially when I am having it dressed, but if it gets alright again I shall have to "keep smiling" The hospital people are most kind to us and the doctor seems to want to do his very best for everybody. The address only stands whilst I am in hospital, afterwards I will let you know my other address.

And now I suppose you will want to know how it happened. If ever anybody was looked after that morning I was. It was July 1st and before we went over the top, I had my ammunition pouch blown clean off my equipment and a hole through my tunic pocket as big as half a crown.

Pte H Fielding *(Mr John Fielding*

As soon as we got over my bayonet was broken clean off, with a bullet I fancy. Them I got hit with shrapnel in the leg (left). Afterwards, I must have been hit again but do not know when. Well, I got into a shell-hole and it was whilst I was taking potshots from there that I was shot through the face.

The bullet entered the left side , between the ear and eye and gashed the back and top of my mouth a little and left at the joint of my right ear, splintering my jaw-bone there. My chum bound it up as best he could but we could not stop it bleeding at my nose and mouth and I lay there until dark.

After dark I crept out and I must have gone round in a circle, because I found myself looking down the barrels of four German rifles, so I threw the sponge up. I was far too fatigued to crawl any further and they treated me very well. I shall never forget that day in that shell-hole but I think I have something to he thankful for that I am alive at all, another inch or so would have done it . The doctor takes the pieces of broken bone out and I think the face will get quite right in time. I can only eat sloppy

*foods yet and have had eggs and milk, rice, etc. with a few
biscuits and jam and tea and coffee. My mouth is not quite as
sore now but I cannot bite.*

*Besides some handkerchiefs I would like some cotton (to sew
my trousers) and needles and a bit of wool to darn the socks,
grey preferred, a few envelopes and a few sheets of notepaper,
also a pencil, if this is not asking too much.*

*This is all for the present, so will close with love to you and
all at '22', also father. Kind remembrances to Miss Harwood
and her mother and Mr. and Mrs. Bates. I can only write two
letters per month now and one post-card per week. One other
thing, Miss Mashiter of Hardman Street sent me a parcel just
before we went into the trenches and I sent a field post-card and
a promise of a letter. It's impossible to write now, so will you
drop her a line and explain things. Miss Harwood will
understand that I cannot write to her.*

Best of Love from Harry.

*'P.S. If Uncle John has an old safety-razor ask him if I can
have it. I have neither money nor belongings.*

Pte Fielding was twenty-one at the time of his capture. When he
returned from Germany he resumed his work as an assistant with H. L.
Baxter Limited, booksellers and music dealers, of Blackburn. (The
Miss Harwood he refers to was another assistant.) Shortly before the

**A group of British prisoners of war at Nurnberg, Bavaria in 1917. Pte
Fielding is second from left on front row. Note the sabots.** *(Mr John Fielding)*

Second World War he bought the business and ran it until his retirement in the 1960s. During the war he served in the Home Guard at Wilpshire, near his home in Salesbury, near Blackburn. He died in 1977, aged 82.

d) *Pte. Fred Sayer – journey to the rear*

On 4 July, the fear of counter-attack over, the remnants of the Pals withdrew to Rolland Trench, in the fourth line of the defences. Later in the day they were relieved by a company of the 6th Gloucestershire Regiment of 144 Brigade, 48th Division. The broken battalion retired to Louvencourt to rest. Some individuals, such as Pte. Sayer, made their own way back:

'On 4 July, which was my nineteenth birthday, we were told we were going to Louvencourt , where Z Company headquarters was now based. I asked Captain Heys, our only surviving officer, if I could leave early and go overland. I think he thought I was barmy but said he would he grateful if I could make it somehow.

'I have made that journey a thousand times since and I still recollect every minute and every yard of the trail which started at two in the afternoon and finished around midnight. The previous day's rain rendered the remains of the trenches too difficult for me to negotiate, so saying "Cheerio! " to my comrades and with a "Good Luck" from Capt. Heys, I left.

'An age later, after working from shell-hole to shell-hole, taking any cover available, I came into the open world. As I passed the remains of the 'Sucrerie' on my left, I came to green fields, with gun emplacements to be out-flanked and avoided, A few 'heavies' were passing overhead,

The first reports of the attack raised false hopes to people at home, The Times, 3 July 1916. *(The Pals Collection)*

"THE DAY GOES WELL."

DETAILS OF THE FIGHTING.

SEMI-OFFICIAL REPORTS.

BRITISH HEADQUARTERS, JULY 1.

9.30 A.M.—British Offensive. At about half-past 7 o'clock this morning a vigorous attack was launched by the British Army. The front extends over about 20 miles north of the Somme. The assault was preceded by a terrific bombardment lasting about an hour and a half.

It is too early as yet to give anything but the barest particulars, as the fighting is developing in intensity, but the British troops have already occupied the German front line.

Many prisoners have already fallen into our hands, and as far as can be ascertained our casualties have not been heavy.

1.15 P.M.—Our troops making good progress into the enemy territory beyond the front line. We have taken Serre and Montauban, two important tactical points respectively to south-east of Hebuterne [north of Albert] and north-east of Bray [on the Somme].

Our troops are fighting in villages of Mametz [east of Fricourt and west of Montauban] and Contalmaison [north of Fricourt], parts of which they hold. We are also holding ground to north of Fricourt [east of Albert and north of Bray], the village itself being still in German hands.

Attacks are being made by us upon Beaumont-Hamel [south of Hebuterne], and we have taken La Boisselle [north of Fricourt].

Our troops are fighting in most gallant manner and many prisoners have been taken in front lines.

The French are advancing on our right with great steadiness and gallantry, and covered very quickly after the assault two kilometres [about 1¼ miles] beyond enemy front line, capturing Curlu [just north of the Somme] and Faviere Wood [south-east of Montauban].

So far the day goes well for England and France.

making a noise like a goods-train as they went on their way to the rear areas. Suddenly, a shell screamed down at me, landing with a hefty thud about fifty yards to my right. I flattened out, but it didn't explode. Deciding that it wasn't for me, I looked down the hole it had made in the ground. It was a nice clean hole about twelve inches across, with the sides sliced by the spin of the shell.

'Just before I reached Colincamps I met two or three platoons of troops. They were moving along in single file and all looked at me. They were all shaved and polished and I felt their sympathy and kindness as we passed on our respective ways.

'Colincamps had been knocked about but the old Brigade H.Q. was still there. I went inside and there was a telephone or signals orderly on duty. He gave me a drink of tea and a chair to rest awhile. Outside I examined my clothes and equipment. The only thing that was clean was my rifle and my leg (which showed through a large tear in my trousers). The rest of me was disgusting. It was remarkable how lice breed in a few days.

'Against the wall of HQ was an army bicycle and knowing there was a long incline on the road to Courcelles, I took it along. Out of the village, I thought that I could free wheel for about a mile and this would be helpful as I could not pedal. It was jolly to be off my feet, and a delightful feeling to be moving without any effort until, I think, I fell asleep. I 'came to' sitting in a deep ditch full of water and greenery and when I sorted

Present day Colincamps, looking east. The war memorial and church.

(The Pals Collection)

myself out, I felt a little cleaner. I left the cycle in the ditch and
proceeded on my weary way.

It was an involuntary action that took me along the roads
through Courcelles, Bertrancourt, Bus, then to Louvencourt to Z
Company H.Q. I developed into a perfect introvert. Although I
was moving steadily towards my goal, I felt tied to a taut but
constraining, invisible force which held me back. In fighting this
negative force I completely ignored any help. I passed several
military units where I could have obtained help and
refreshments. The darkness intensified the feeling and instinct
alone kept me on the right track to Louvencourt.

'Suddenly I was surrounded by men from H.Q. who were
waiting to guide us to billets. They took my rifle and equipment
and led me into a barn which had several storm-lamps burning
and straw on the earthen floor. There were blankets. I don't
remember eating any food, but I well remember tea - I drank and
drank. I, or someone, stripped off my uniform, or what was left
of it, and I was down on a glorious bed. It was fresh straw
purchased from the farmer by H.Q. (the first time they had ever
done this for us). No four-poster bed with eider-downs and all
the glories of the castle bed-chamber ever had a more
appreciative sleeper than that humble straw had. I slept for nine
hours.

'When I awoke about twenty others were there. We were given
breakfast in bed, or at least where we had slept. The barn doors
were open and the sunlight streamed in. All was peaceful.
Nobody spoke. There were no N.C.O.s or officers. Gradually we
eased ourselves outside. We quietly washed ourselves down, then
sat on the barn foundation stones to scrape the mud and grime
of battle from our equipment.

'It was a sober moment for all of us. About one in five of us
were left and many of these, like me, were not fit for duty. We
talked quietly, trying to ascertain what had happened. We had
trained together for nearly two years and someone had messed
things up and we had paid the price. There was much sadness at
our failure and, for once, "humour" – that paragon of the
British Army – was absent.'

On 6 July the survivors of the Battalion marched from Louvencourt to
Gezaincourt where they stayed two days. Percy Crabtree found time to
sketch his billet. The 1998 scene is much changed apart from the
tower.

On 6 July the survivors of the Battalion marched to Gezaincourt where they stayed two days. L/Cpl Crabtree found time to paint his billet. *(The Liddle Collection)*

The 1998 scene is much changed apart from the **tower.** *(The Pals Collection)*

Following the Trail

Private Sayer's journey to Louvencourt can be followed by car. The most practical **start-point** is where the **D919 Mailly – Maillet** to **Serre** road crosses the **D28/D174 Hebuterne** to **Auchonvillers** road. The ruined sugar-beet refinery (the Sucrerie) which marked the entrance to 94 Brigade's trench system was nearby. *'I passed the remains of the Sucrerie to my left'*.

Some 300 yards (275 metres) to the left of the crossroads is Sucrerie Military Cemetery. The approach is by a long, narrow, track, just wide enough for a car. There are 894 graves, of which four are of

Pals. Two, Private Clarke and L/Cpl. Hartley, were buried on 29/4/1916, the first Pals to be killed in action. Pte's Jackson and Pickering were killed by accident a month later (see page 30).

Private Sayer would first go towards Colincamps along the D174, Hebuterne, road before bearing left onto the D129E. On the roadside to the left would be the site of Euston Road Cemetery. A light railway then ran nearby bringing supplies to the front-line at Railway Hollow. (When 2/Lt. Bart Endean arrived at the Battalion in April 1916, his first job was to organise the construction nearby of Euston Dump, after which the cemetery was named). The cemetery now contains 1261 graves, many of which were concentrated there after the war. There are 26 Pals, all killed in action on 1/7/1916.

In Colincamps is the *Mairie*, now rebuilt, in which, in 1916, was 94 Brigade HQ. It was from outside this building that Private Sayer 'borrowed' the bicycle. Near the junction with the D129 Sailly-au-Bois road are barns and farm buildings which, in 1916, were used as billets. At the junction turn right, then left, onto the unclassified road which goes directly to Courcelles. In 1916 the right hand side of the road was strung with camouflage nets to hamper the observation by the enemy of troop movements. If one looks towards Serre and the old front line one can understand why they were necessary. It was down this road that Private Sayer free-wheeled on his borrowed bicycle.

On entering Courcelles, **bear left onto the D114** road to Bertrancourt. (Just to the right, on the road to Sailly-au-Bois, is the Communal Cemetery and Extension. Of the total of 115 war graves there is one Pal – Private Taylor – who died of wounds on 13/11/1916). Go through the village and on to the straight **road to Bertrancourt**. At

'I passed the remains of the Sucrerie to my left', Fred Sayer's journey to the rear. *(The Pals Collection)*

the village, **turn right onto the D176E** road to Cogneux. As the road leaves Bertrancourt, **turn left on to the D176**. About 400 yards (365 metres) west of Bertrancourt is Bertrancourt Military Cemetery. 416 men are recorded in the register, of whom there are 13 Pals who died in June 1916).

The D176 is a short, winding road leading into Bus-les-Artois. Behind the church is Bois du Bus (Bus Wood), in 1916 the site of a hutted encampment. In the **centre** of the village **turn left** onto the open, unclassified, road to Louvencourt. It was at the entrance to the village that the HQ staff were waiting to lead Private Sayer and other survivors of the failed assault, to their billets in the ruined barn.

It is estimated that the total length of Private Sayer's walk from the front line, through Colincamps, Courcelles, Bertrancourt and Bus-les-Artois to Louvencourt was something like nine miles – say fifteen kilometres. His journey time then was approximately ten hours.

Walks (and car tours) around the area of the Serre battlefield are extremely well covered in a special chapter (pp 103 – 136) of *Serre*, by Jack Horsfall and Nigel Cave. One of the **Battleground Europe** series, this is published by Pen & Sword Books, (1996).

Another useful book is *Walking the Somme*, by Paul Reed (same publisher, 1997), in which the area is described in more general terms as part of a guide for those touring the battlefields on foot.

4. *Casualties and Awards*
CASUALTIES

Nine officers and 228 men were killed as a result of the attack. As far as is known, twelve officers and 339 men were wounded. At least seventeen men died of their wounds in the weeks following. This brings the total of 254 officers and men who died, and 351 wounded, to 605.

136 of those who died are commemorated on the Thiepval Memorial. 118 are buried in a total of fifteen cemeteries in France and England. 50 lie in Queen's Cemetery, Puisieux; 24 in Euston Road

Serre Road Cemetery No 2, Beaumont Hamel, Hebuterne. A view from the rear. *(Mr Bob Curley)*

Cemetery, Colincamps; 15 in Railway Hollow Cemetery, Hebuterne; 6 in Serre Road Cemetery No.3, Puisieux and 3 in Serre Road Cemetery No.2, Beaumont-Hamel. There are one each in Beaumont-Hamel British Cemetery and Serre Road Cemetery No.1, Hebuterne. 15362 Pte. Arthur Dent lies in Tilloy British Cemetery, south east of Arras. He was, presumably, captured by the Germans and died of his wounds

Of the seventeen men noted as 'died of wounds', five were buried in Doullens Communal Cemetery Extension; two in

The Thiepval Memorial. *(Mr Bob Curley)*

Beauval Communal Cemetery; two in St. Pol British Cemetery, and one each in St. Sever Cemetery, Rouen and Etretat Churchyard, near Le Havre.

In England, five men who died in English hospitals lie in Accrington Cemetery and there is one man in Padiham Cemetery, near Burnley. In all a total of 254.

It cannot be said precisely how many died or were wounded as a result of 1 July. For those killed in action and died of wounds the above figures are based on the registers of the Commonwealth War Graves Commission. The figures for those wounded are from the Battalion War Diary. No count can be made, of course, of those who died as a result of their wounds anything up to twenty or more years later. Therefore these figures must be considered as minimal.

The casualties sustained by the Battalion as a result of 1 July 1916 were the largest ever suffered in any action. This experience changed the Battalion from a local, almost parochial, unit of inexperienced enthusiasts to a battle-hardened force equal to, if not better than, many infantry battalions on the Western Front. Thus they served, always with gallantry and honour, throughout the rest of the war.

Even the totals on Thiepval Memorial must be considered as minimal. The name of 17840 Pte. Joseph Riley of Church, was added in 1998.

AWARDS

As far as is known one Military Cross, three Distinguished Conduct Medals and three Military Medals were awarded for acts of bravery on 1 July.

Lt. Thomas William Rawcliffe was awarded the M.C. for his deter-

47

Lt T W Rawcliffe MC.
(The Pals Collection)

mination and coolness when bringing four trench mortars into position through a very heavy barrage.

15183 C.S.M. Arthur Leeming handled his company with great coolness and skill when all his officers became casualties.

15961 L/Cpl Esmond Nowell, although wounded, delivered a message to H.Q. through heavy fire and then returned to his company. Nowell later won the Military Medal whilst serving with 2 East Lancashire Regiment.

17992 Pte. William Warburton single-handedly attacked an enemy bombing party in a German communication trench. He killed an officer, wounded others and caused the remainder to retire. All the above men were each awarded the D.C.M.

The following three men were awarded the M.M. :

18048 Pte. Stanley M. Bewsher reached a German communication trench and fired his Lewis gun at a group of the enemy forcing them to retire. When his own gun was damaged by shellfire, he picked up another and continued his attack.

15657 Sgt. Austin Lang was killed whilst leading his men, after his officers became casualties, in the attack on the enemy trenches. (awarded posthumously). Sgt. Lang's body was never found or identified and his name is commemorated on the Thiepval Memorial.

24139 Pte. Holford Speak, although wounded, left the safety of a shell hole to assist a wounded comrade. He was immediately wounded a second time but both he and his comrade were able to return to their own lines.

5. Re-organisation of the stretcher-bearers – July

Later in July Pte. Sayer was informed by Major Kershaw (newly promoted) that he was to train the Battalion's new stretcher-bearers.

"'I can't do it, Sir, I'm a bomber". "Nonsense!, I know you were a doctor's pupil before you enlisted. You used to treat my wife's mother in Burnley. If you can do that you can teach first-aid."'

On that slender basis, Pte. Sayer became L/Cpl. Sayer, Medical

Cpl Harrison (i/c water), Pte Webster (MO's batman), L/Cpl Crabtree and L/Cpl Sayer. Photograph taken in France 1916. *(Mrs J Langton)*

Orderly, with responsibility for thirty-two stretcher-bearers.

Pte. Percy Crabtree was a volunteer. Fred Sayer interviewed him:

'My enquiry as to first-aid brought the reply "Teachers need to know a little". I promptly accepted him. At my suggestion, Percy was given a stripe and put in charge of the stretcher-bearers.'

'Percy Crabtree was a product of his own efforts which gave him college training and ten years teaching experience. He was a delightful fellow, quite unsuitable for army life, but fitting in and making the best of every situation. He had lots of patience, a subtle sense of humour, a love of music and he was a painter in water colours. His job now was to organise the stretcher-bearers.'

'Captain Anglin, a Canadian, our Medical Officer, was responsible for the health of the Battalion and was supposed to keep an eye on food, water and sanitation. I, as Medical Orderly, was responsible for the sick and wounded, organising the

The stretcher bearers and medical staff. L/Cpl Sayer is on the Medical Officer's left, L/Cpl Crabtree is on his right. *(Mrs J Langton)*

THE
BATTALION
CHIROPODIST.

movement of equipment and supplies to and from the line and for the training of the stretcher-bearers. There was a Sergeant Cook, a Water Corporal, a Sanitary Corporal, a Chiropody L/Cpl. and a Stretcher-Bearer L/Cpl. Apart from the latter, the rest did not concern me, except that the Water Corporal and the Chiropodist joined the M.O.s batman and attached themselves to our squad.

'This was the gathering together of a group based on mutual support in feeding, entertainment and morale, although Percy's singing and harmony might have been the attraction. We became very fond of a little sing-song, much to Percy's delight.'

6. Thoughts on trench names – Percy Crabtree

'We marched from Warnimont Wood to Colincamps and the front line. It was Monday – washing day in the French villages evidently as in Burnley. But what a day! A fine drizzle finished up as pouring rain, and we were well soaked as we filed down Du Guesclin trench, along Jean Bart to the front line, the left

Sketches by L/Cpl Crabtree.
(The Liddle Collection)

Corporal Harrison

50

flank resting on John Copse of ill-omen.

'Here were some old trenches named by the French when they held this line in 1915. **Vercingtorix** – an old Gaulish chieftain who fought the Romans almost to a standstill, but was later captured to grace a Roman triumph in the Eternal City. **Du Guesclin** – a famous old French knight who grimly fought the English on this same soil several centuries ago. **Jean Bart** – pirate and privateersman, who harried English shipping in those years of interminable warfare when France was the old enemy. Oddly enough, we were all glad to have the shelter and protection of old Jean Bart, reprobate though he was, in our journeys to the front line.

'How different were the English in their naming of trenches and how significant of the temperamental and racial differences between French and English. The Battalion occupied **Blind Alley**, **Jam Street**, **Pub Trench** – all in this area. Nothing to rouse the martial spirit there, like **Jena** a communication trench named after one of Napoleon's greatest victories.

'Only the profane and sacrilegious English could have named four small copses after four apostles – **Matthew**, **Mark**, **Luke** and **John**.'

7. Bitten on the Bottom – by Fred Sayer

'This part of the line was supposed to be a quiet one. One day, however, the Boche sent over some heavy stuff onto a working party in a communication trench and they buried the party with the first salvo. It was a ghastly business and it turned the head of the Sergeant Major in charge. He went berserk and was going towards the Boche line with bayonet fixed, when someone grabbed him. He was brought to the Aid Post along with many badly wounded. The little place was full to overflowing, and there was a great commotion with the S.M. trampling over wounded men trying to "get at em". He was just above me and I saw he was just plain crazy, so I hit him on the jaw and he quietly subsided across a poor fellow lying on a stretcher.

'I was sitting on an improvised cot which already contained a badly wounded man, but I managed to push him over and put the unconscious S.M. alongside him. I then sat on the S.M.'s chest and carried on applying first aid and writing labels, so that lightly wounded could get away. Suddenly I was bitten on the bottom. I nearly jumped through the roof. Fortunately khaki

Battalion stretcher bearers take a casualty to the Aid Post. *(The Liddle Collection)*

uniforms are quite thick but the S.M. had a good voice and some hefty teeth. I dare not knock him out again, so I rendered him harmless by tying up his arms and his legs.

'It was hours before we got back to normal and as the last of the wounded was carried away we stretcher-bearers gathered at the Aid Post. The heavy pressures had left us all limp and weary. Suddenly someone said "What about your wound, Corporal?" There was a silence, then – "He's been bit in the backside by the Sergeant Major!" The tension departed as everyone roared with laughter and demanded I had my stern cauterised. it was a merry five minutes of real army humour which ended in comments of what would happen to me when I was court-martialled for knocking out a warrant officer. Tears flowed because of the hilarious situation, laughter came easily and was welcome as a relief valve.'

8. Hot Tea – by Fred Sayer

'The situation was crazy. We had nothing but our hands (usually frozen) and sandbags to help half-frozen wounded survive a wait of perhaps four hours before they reached the field hospital. I suggested to the M.O. that there should be hot drinks of either tea or meat extract for the sick and wounded. He looked a little suspicious and said "It's not laid on , but what do you

suggest?" "Leave it to me, Sir!".

'*Off I went to see the Quarter Master. I knew him in Civvy Street and waited for him to be alone. I sort of claimed privilege and talked to him on equal terms. All I had to do was to dramatise the case of one man, whom we both knew, who had just left us, wounded, cold and weary. He said, "It's a matter of supplies." I suggested that it was worth it if all the HQ staff had to do without tea, but we had lost thirty men in our last spell and he was still drawing their rations. The Q.M. had no answer to that and suddenly there was no problem. I left with two full sandbags, one tea and one sugar, plus tins of milk.*

'*What a blessing! And also given with the blessing of the Quarter Master, which meant that future supplies were assured.*

'*I am sure this humble treatment saved many lives. The joy a wounded man showed when given a hot drink was unbelievable. The stretcher bearers, whose job was a pretty tough one, needed to be revived and often a hot drink made possible another trip. We in the Aid Post enjoyed testing each drink to see that it was not too hot. We could not afford to let our spirits flag.*'

9. Following the 1916 Trail of the Pals

Most British visitors to the Somme battlefields arrive in France either at Calais ferry terminal or the Channel Tunnel terminal. There is then a choice of routes. Firstly, via the Paris A26-E15 Autoroute past Arras, then to Bapaume on the A1-E15 (junction 14). Secondly, there is the A16 Autoroute to Amiens, thence to Albert on the D929.

If one has the time however, the drive from Calais or Boulogne to, and through, the towns of Montreuil, Hesdin, Frevent and Doullens and from there through the rear areas of the old front line is relatively pleasant. It is also much more rewarding because from Doullens one follows the trail of the Pals to Serre through the villages and countryside with which they were familiar in 1916 and 1917.

A personal choice is to take the *N1 towards Boulogne,* then continue on the N1 to Montreuil. From there take the N39 to Hesdin. This road goes through the very pleasant, and quiet, valley of the River Canche. From Hesdin continue along the valley on the D340 to Frevent. This brings one to the D916 and onto Doullens. Doullens was an important base throughout the war. Its position well behind the lines, at the meeting of roads from St. Pol, Arras, Amiens and Albert made it a very important transportation centre.

On the drive to the battlefield it may be appropriate to consider several detours, which could be included in a personal itinerary. (see map 1)

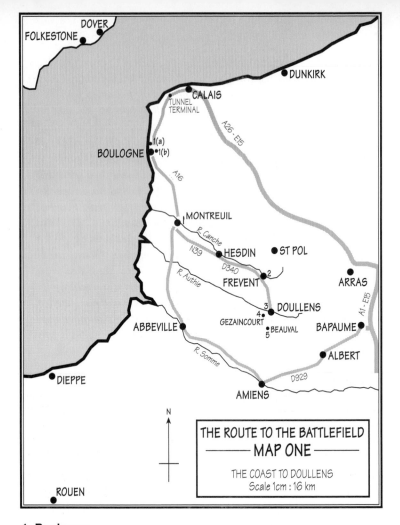

THE ROUTE TO THE BATTLEFIELD
— MAP ONE —

THE COAST TO DOULLENS
Scale 1cm : 16 km

1. Boulogne

(a) Two miles north of the town is Terlincthun British Cemetery, Wimille. The cemetery contains the graves of men and women who died of wounds or sickness (mostly influenza) in nearby hospitals. The cemetery is still 'open', in that it is used for the burial of bodies still found on the old battlefields of France. Twelve Pals are buried here. Eight died of Influenza, or its complications, whilst four died of wounds. 15860 Pte. Andrew MacGrath, who caught pneumonia after celebrating the Armistice, died on 21 November 1918. His grave is in Plot X1 Row C Grave 26. Nearby in X1 C32 is 2/Lt. Mark Thomas Washbrook who died on the same day from wounds sustained on 18 October 1918 at Wattrelos, near Roubaix.

(b) On the high ground overlooking the town is Boulogne Eastern Cemetery. The register records 5,578 burials. Three Pals who died of wounds in local hospitals are here. One died in November 1916 and two who were wounded near Hazebrouck at the end of April 1918.

2. Frevent

The Communal Cemetery of St. Hilaire is on the eastern side of the town. Here are three Pals who died of wounds sustained at Ayette in the German March 1918 Offensive. They were amongst the last to be buried in the cemetery before the Extension was opened.

3. Doullens

Up to April 1918 men who died of wounds at the Casualty Clearing Stations based in the medieval Citadelle were buried in an Extension (No. 1) to the nearby Communal Cemetery. Five Pals, all but one wounded on 1 July 1916, lie here.

4. Gezaincourt

Between Doullens and the village is Gezaincourt Communal Cemetery and Extension. There are 590 graves in the Extension, one of which is of 15505 Pte. Percy Hargreaves who died of wounds on 26 June 1916. From 5 to 13 June 1916 the village was the scene of full-scale Brigade rehearsals for the 1 July attack.

5. Beauval

Beauval is a large village four miles (6.5kms.) south of Doullens on the N25 road to Amiens. The Communal Cemetery is on the northern side, at the end of a cul-de-sac. Four Pals are buried here. Two died of wounds received on 1 July 1916 and one died of appendicitis on 26 May. 20927 Pte. Arthur Riley, who died of wounds on 30 April, lies in

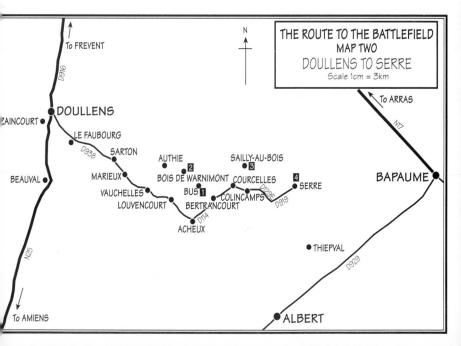

THE ROUTE TO THE BATTLEFIELD
MAP TWO
DOULLENS TO SERRE
Scale 1cm = 3km

Sarton Church in 1998.
(The Pals Collection)

Sarton Church as painted by L/Cpl Crabtree during a halt on the march in 1916. *(The Liddle Collection)*

grave E7. He was the first Pal to die on active service in France. After living in Rhode Island, U.S.A., for several years he returned to Accrington in July 1915 to enlist.

Continuing **from Doullens, turn south onto the N16**, the Amiens road. On the outskirts of the town **turn left** onto the **D938**, sign-posted to Albert. This road follows the very picturesque valley of the River Authie. This is a pleasant run, in complete contrast to the busy N16. This quiet road passes by numbers of roadside bungalows and small houses, many with gardens, until one reaches the appropriately named hamlet of le Faubourg (the outskirts), some two and a half miles (4kms) from Doullens. From there to Sarton it is three miles (5kms.).

As with most villages in the area there is a peaceful, almost lethargic, air about Sarton. This is in contrast to the war years, when it was at an important road junction in the rear area. It was in constant use as billets and as a depot for line of communication troops. It also served as a resting place for troops going to and from the front line. The D938 continues past Vauchelles-les-Authie to Louvencourt, thirteen miles (21kms.) from Doullens.

On 1 July Louvencourt was six miles (11kms.) behind the front line. It was here, on 4 July, that the survivors of the Pals assembled after the battle. Just at the end of the village a narrow unclassified road (easily missed) meets the D938. Down this road, on the left, is Louvencourt Military Cemetery.

This is the first 'cemetery stop' for many visitors en-route to the battlefields. There are seventy-five French and 151 British war graves. 2/Lt. Roland Aubrey Leighton of 7 Worcester Regiment who died of wounds on 23 December 1915, is buried in grave I B 20. Primroses mark the grave. 2/Lt . Leighton was the friend of Vera Brittain, the author of *Testament of Youth*, a classic memoir of the period. Also here, in grave I F 9 is Brigadier General C. B. Prowse, Commander of 11 Brigade, 4th Division, the most senior officer to be killed on 1 July 1916. There are no Pals in this cemetery.

Follow the D938 to the larger village of Acheux-en-Amienois. In 1916 Acheux was a forward base and railhead for much of the *matériel* needed for the front. 8 Corps Walking Wounded Collection Centre was here and Ambulance Trains used the station to take wounded to Doullens.

Turn left onto the **D114 to Bertrancourt**, three miles (5kms.) to the northeast. In the months before 1 July the village was used as billets for the Pals and other troops whilst in 31st Divisional Reserve. A Main Dressing Station was based here. Some four hundred yards (365 metres) up a narrow lane is Bertrancourt Military Cemetery. Twelve Pals killed during the last tour of duty in the front line before 1 July (19 to 24 June) are buried here. 16043 Pte. Arthur Nutter, who died in a training accident on 17 June, lies in grave I D 18.

From Bertrancourt it is a short drive to Courcelles-au-Bois. From March to June 1916 the village was used by the Pals and others as billets when in 94 Brigade Reserve. The Mairie (the Town Hall) became Battalion HQ Courcelles was therefore in constant use as an assembly point for battalions on their way into, or out of, the front line. The whole area was full of British artillery positions and consequently was the target for German retaliatory shellfire. On 1 July 1916 the village was the site of 31st Division HQ

The Communal Cemetery and Extension is on the northern edge of the village at the junction of the unclassified road to Coigneux and the D114 to Sailly-au-Bois. The Extension was started in October 1916 and

The Mairie in Courcelles. *(The Pals Collection)*

Colincamps looking West. *(The Pals Collection)*

used until March 1917 and again in 1918. 29479 Pte. Edgar Taylor, who died of wounds received near Hebuterne on 13 November 1916, lies in grave C 7. (Pte. Taylor was one of forty men who died during the period 19 October 1916 to 18 March 1917 in the Battalion's tour of duty in the nearby Hebuterne / Sailly-au-Bois sector).

Just before the cemetery, however, a narrow unclassified road, signposted to Colincamps, turns sharply to the right (another easily missed). The road rises over open ground. In 1916 there was a screen of camouflage netting alongside the left side of the road. One understands why when one considers the numbers of troops using this road to and from the front line, and the open view of the area from the German front line at Serre and beyond.

It is just over half a mile (1km.) to Colincamps. The village, like so many others in the area, is quiet, with an almost deserted air. During the war however, it was completely destroyed. It was, in 1916, well known to the Pals. It was the last village before going into the trenches before Serre. 15139 Pte. George Pollard, then seventeen, remembered his first visit 'We were in a barn, with tiers of wooden bunks. We walked about the streets, gazing round at the wreckage. We thought how wonderful it was to be at the Front'.

The barn is in the farmyard on the left as one enters the village on the road from Courcelles. The Ecole (School) was used as Battalion HQ during their stays in the village. (In 1920, Burnley, home town of Z Company, adopted Colincamps and Courcelles and helped finance the rebuilding of the villages).

Continue **out of Colincamps** down the **D129E** (signposted to Auchonvillers), to Euston Road Cemetery, half a mile (800 metres) on the right. The cemetery was used during and after the 1 July battles. The register records 1,261 names, of which twenty-six are Pals. All were killed in action on 1 July.

58

Continue to the **junction with the D919** at la Fabrique Farm. This is the site of the Sucrerie from which troops going into the front line entered the trench system. On the Mailly-Maillet side of the D919 is the access road to Sucrerie Military Cemetery. There are 894 graves here, four of which are of Pals. Two died in April 1916 and two were killed accidentally in May.

When returning from the cemetery, turn left onto the D919 towards Serre and Puisieux. Along the road to the right is Serre Road Cemetery No.2. This is the largest cemetery on the Somme, with 7,139 graves. Three Pals are of this number. Whilst continuing towards Serre one comes to the French National Cemetery on the left. Nearby is Serre Road Cemetery No.1 24514 Pte. John Winter is buried in grave V C 9. The original cemetery was made in 1917 and was greatly enlarged after the Armistice by the concentration here of bodies found in different parts of the battlefield. Pte. Winter would be one of these.

On leaving the cemetery **turn left** towards Serre, but t**urn left almost immediately** where a C.W.G.C. sign directs visitors up a track to the Serre battlefield. Serre Road Cemetery No.3 is at the top of the slope. It is in the open field on the site of the German front line. Eighty-one men lie here. Six are Pals who died on 1 July.

Continue along the track across the old No Man's Land to Mark Copse. This is the place from which the Pals advanced on 1 July. The Accrington Pals Memorial is just behind what was then the second line trench (the first line trench was filled in many years ago). There were originally four copses – Matthew, Mark, Luke and John – but Matthew Copse was ploughed over after the war.

Behind Mark and Luke Copses is Railway Hollow Cemetery. The Cemetery is on the site of the Regimental Aid Post used on 1 July. Fifteen Pals are buried here. In common with many cemeteries on the Somme – and indeed the Western Front – there are also graves of men

Serre Road Cemetery No. 3. *(The Pals Collection)*

'Known unto God'. These are men unidentified at the time of burial. 73,357 such men died in the Somme battles between July 1915 and March 1918. Their memorial at Thiepval names 145 Pals.

As one returns to the British front line past the memorial shelter of Sheffield Memorial Park, there is a path across the field to Queen's Cemetery. There are 312 graves, fifty of which are of named Pals. All the Pals died on 1 July but were not buried until the cemetery was formed in May 1917.

It is here that this Trail must end. If by a miracle any Pals got into Serre village nothing is known about them. The few prisoners taken by the Germans appear to have been picked up in No Man's Land after the attack failed. It seems appropriate, therefore, that this journey to the battlefield ends at this place, the furthest the Pals advanced that day. In common with the first part of the journey, several detours can be made if time permits:

The second line trench and The Pals Memorial. *(The Pals Collection)*

1. Bus-les-Artois

The village is on the D176 some one and a quarter miles (2kms.) northwest from Bertrancourt. (There is an alternative way, slightly longer, from Louvencourt, along an unclassified road). Bus is a quiet, pleasant place, in a well wooded valley. The Bois de Bus (Bus Wood) is on the northern edge of the village. In 1916 there were hutted camps in the wood. These were used as a rest camp and a base for working

Mark and Luke copses and the Sheffield Memorial from Queen's Cemetery. *(Mr Bob Curley)*

parties. There is no trace now that hundreds of men were billeted here at any one time. The wood is privately owned.

2. The Bois de Warnimont (Warnimont Wood)

The wood is alongside the D176 on the way from Bus to Authie. In 1916 the wood was full of huts and tents. When newly built in the Spring of 1916 it was described as 'an idyllic setting' but it rapidly became very muddy and unpleasant. The Pals were here when in Divisional Reserve. Pte. Pollard described their accommodation as 'wretched, with neither doors nor windows, nor beds to sleep on'. It was from Warnimont Wood, on 30 June, that the Pals began their seven mile march to the trenches at Serre. They used the woods again as a rest area during the months from October 1916 to February 1917 in their second tour of duty in the area. There is now no trace of any military occupation. This wood is also privately owned.

3. Sailly-au-Bois

Sailly is on the D114 just over a mile (2kms) northeast of Courcelles. It is a similar distance on the D129 from Colincamps. During the Somme battles the area was full of artillery positions, and the village was eventually destroyed by German shellfire. During their second tour of duty on the Somme, from October 1916 to February 1917, the Pals used a hutted camp in Sailly Dell, on the western edge of the village, when out of the line. Sailly-au-Bois Military Cemetery is also on the western edge of the village, on

(The Liddle Collection)

the D23 to Bayencourt. The cemetery was begun in May 1916 and used by Field Ambulances until March 1917. It was used again in 1918. The register records 239 burials, of which twelve are Pals. Five died in November and seven on 31 December 1916.

The church at Sailly-au-Bois in 1916 and 1998. *(The Pals Collection)*

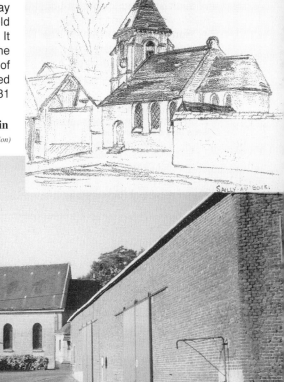

German positions in Serre destroyed by shell fire. Photograph taken in February 1917.

4. Serre

The tiny village of Serre is on the D919 road from Mailly-Maillet to Puisieux which is a mile and a half (2.5kms.) to the north. Serre is smaller now than it was in 1916. Its position on relatively high open ground helps to explain how, and why, it was so strongly held by the Germans against every attack. Three major attempts to take Serre failed. The first, by French troops in June 1915, cost them approximately 2,000 men killed and 9,000 wounded and missing. The second attempt was on 1 July 1916. The third, in which the Pals also had a role, was in November 1916. These three attacks on this village of such strategic importance cost an estimated twenty thousand men killed, wounded and missing.

Serre was never taken. The Germans evacuated it, in their own time, on 24 February 1917 when they moved back to ready-made positions in the Hindenberg Line.

Useful maps are:
1. *Michelin Carte Routiere et Touristique* No. 236 Nord Flandres – Artois – Picardie 1/200000 – 1cm.: 2km.
2. Cartes I.G.N. France (Institute Geographique National).
Serie Bleu 23.07 est Doullens
          24.07 ouest Bapaume
          24.07 est Bapaume.
          1/25000 – 4cm.: 1km.

General view of Serre village. *(The Pals Collection)*

CHAPTER THREE

A Relatively Quiet Year:
January 1917 - December 1917

1. Billets

In the Battalion War Diary and in both Percy Crabtree's and Fred Sayer's reminiscences the phrase 'in billets' is frequently used. This could mean anything from barrack-rooms to wooden huts or bell-tents, but occasionally 'billets' brought troops into contact with the local population. Here are two, rather different, such experiences:

a.) Fred Sayer:

  'Some of us took over a dilapidated cottage with a cellar and a stable. We each laid claim to our pitches and then went on the scrounge. One chap found a barrel of cider and it was not long before the rest of the fellows were sitting round the barrel singing happily until a few became quite merry. It was potent stuff for those who hadn't tasted anything stronger than greasy tea for a long time. They wondered what other troops had been doing to miss the cider.

  'Later our two sergeants found a locked bedroom door. A little push – and it opened. There was great excitement as we all peeped in for here was a bed and bits of lace and a dressing table. Everything had a feminine appearance. The two decided they would rest where angels dwelt and, ignoring the somewhat indelicate remarks of the others, they slammed the door in their faces.

  'A scream in the still, calm, night made everybody sit up in alarm. All was dark where we were but through the cracks in the

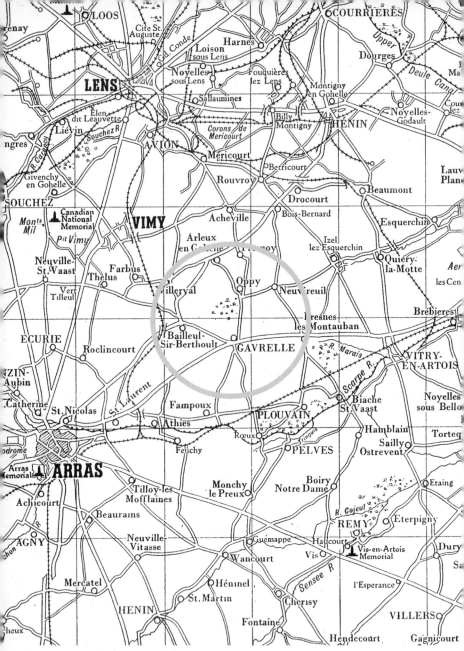

Oppy and Gavrelle in relation to Arras and Vimy Ridge.

Scale 1cm = 2km

bedroom door came rays of light and the most abusive language it was possible to hear. "Mademoiselle from Armentieres has come on a visit", said one humorist and every one roared. The poor sergeants were fast asleep when the lady of the house entered by the outside door. As she lit the lamp, they sat up in bed, and who got the biggest shock is known only to the trio.

'Eventually the real tenant departed and then came the reckoning. A watch, trinkets and what-nots were said to be stolen. Lt. Lewino, our platoon officer, and a French interpreter 'managed' things and the lady got a lot of cash. Incidentally, the cider had to be paid for as well.'

b) Fred Sayer:

'The nearest I had ever seen of French home life was having a coffee in some broken down cottage. One day Percy had fascinated the farmer, whose pig-sty we were sleeping in, by painting the house in water colours. The farmer, who was called Jean, and his wife, Martha, admired the painting and Percy got a chance to practice his French. He came away with some fresh vegetables, then asked Martha if she would cook them. The farmer, standing nearby, said "Yes". Percy followed this up by suggesting "A chicken, perhaps?". Jean sent his wife, who was over sixty, chasing around the farmyard after a very lively chicken. Poor thing, it did not like the idea, but with Percy's help, it was caught. Martha was ordered to execute the bird and get it ready for the table. Next, Percy asked the pair to join us in

'Our billet', a farmhouse in Ligny-sur-Canche painted by L/Cpl Crabtree. *(The Liddle Collection)*

our lunch of the bird and the vegetables.

'*Jean could say "Yes!" quite well and he told his wife, in French, to get busy. He hardly moved an inch all the time. Poor Martha did everything. Even inside the house the farmer just sat and she chased around. The kitchen where we had the meal was large and bare with a flagged floor, rather like the farms in the Yorkshire dales. We all washed and brushed up to enjoy the feast. It was an occasion, because it was a return to civilisation and one to remember, even if the bird was a bit tough. One did not kill a bird and cook it right away. It had to mature, all my country experience told me so.*

'*On a large bare table was a pile of good soup plates, with knives, forks and spoons laid out. In the centre was an enormous blue and white tureen. This contained a clear soup, with bits of parsley floating picturesquely over some minute carrots. It was the vegetable water with something like wine added and it was delicious. Lumps of crusty French bread were passed around, again delicious. Martha almost blushed as we caught her eye and exercised our bit of French.*

'*The next tureen was full of mixed root vegetables. We just helped ourselves, using our soup plates. A small piece of pork fat, about one inch square, was given to each of us and, copying our host, we anointed each vegetable as we ate it. The pieces of chicken followed and, in spite of everything, it was quite good.*

'*Good as the chicken was, the pride of place, after Martha, was the tureen of fresh vegetables. The farmer and his wife enjoyed the party. I do not think they had entertained soldiers before and I guess Percy presented them with the water colour.*

'*Before we left, Jean gave an order to Martha, she smiled brightly and disappeared. From the cellar she brought a bottle of cognac. Jean looked at it, grunted, and she opened it and carefully poured a little into each glass. A solemn toast was drunk. What we pledged I don't know, but my praise and admiration went out to Martha.*'

2. The Long March

On 14 March 1917 the whole of 31st Division commenced a march northwards from the Somme battlefields to the First Army area and by 25 March were billeted in the area around St. Venant. The Division again became part of XIII Corps.

94 Brigade moved off on 25 March and arrived at Merville on the

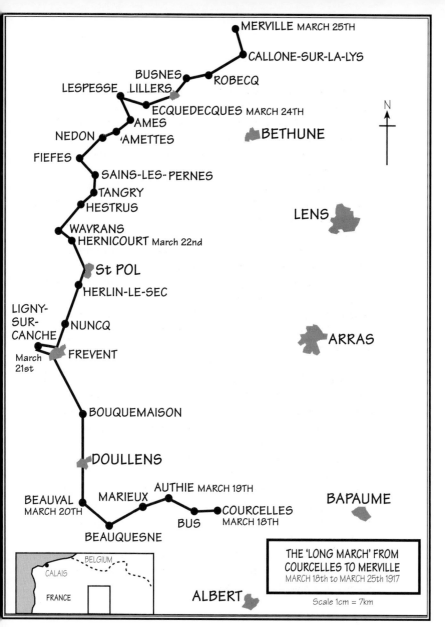

THE 'LONG MARCH' FROM
COURCELLES TO MERVILLE
MARCH 18th to MARCH 25th 1917

Scale 1cm = 7km

25th. With the rest of 31st Division it remained in the area until 8 April
when it moved to the area between Bethune and Arras. A fortnight was
then spent in training for the forthcoming operations in the Oppy –
Gavrelle sector.

On 30 April the Pals moved to Maroeuil in readiness for front line operations at Oppy – but before then, a more personal version of events.

The Battalion War Diary entry for the week, 18 - 25 March 1917, states simply, 'Battalion moved to First Army area by march route, billeting at the places below on the dates shown'. There follows a list of seven places and seven dates.

L/Cpl. Crabtree described the march a little more fully:

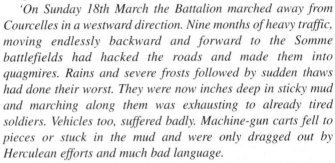

'On Sunday 18th March the Battalion marched away from Courcelles in a westward direction. Nine months of heavy traffic, moving endlessly backward and forward to the Somme battlefields had hacked the roads and made them into quagmires. Rains and severe frosts followed by sudden thaws had done their worst. They were now inches deep in sticky mud and marching along them was exhausting to already tired soldiers. Vehicles too, suffered badly. Machine-gun carts fell to pieces or stuck in the mud and were only dragged out by Herculean efforts and much bad language.

'The night was spent at Authie and on the morrow the march was resumed. Familiar ground this, through Marieux, Beauquesne to Beauval, where the old billets were used again.

'On the next day, March 20th, breakfast was served at 6.30 a.m. A quick clean up and then off on the road north. Doullens was reached in little over an hour. The little old town was basking in wintry sunshine but it was too full of redcaps and staff cars for our taste. "March to attention" was the order here. On we went past the ancient citadel, over the River Authie, past the level crossing near the railway station, then we began to climb from the valley on to the small hills to the north.

'Two miles further on stood an old windmill with arms lazily turning, a fine peaceful sight after the horrors of Beaumont-Hamel. Just beyond this began the long straggling village of Bouquemaison with several inviting estaminets which were forbidden to us marching troops.

'Another halt, and a dumping of packs. The rising blue smoke of cigarettes marked the line of resting men until whistles blew and the march continued over the moorlands to Frevent, a small town lying in the valley of the River Canche.

'This seemed a natural halting place for the night but the higher powers ordained otherwise, we trudged on to Ligny-sur-Canche, a mile or so to the west. A sick parade was held at about 5.30 p.m. and a few men with badly blistered feet were given a

A not untypical scene on the country roads behind the line. *(Taylor Library)*

*chit to ride with the transport the next day. We 'Z' Company men
were billeted in a farm nearly 300 years old – and it smelt so.*

'The next morning, the 21st, the sun rose brightly, augury of
a fine day. We were all beginning to enjoy this march. Down by
the river French wives were washing clothes and some wag
called out "Hey, missus, will ye wash my socks?" We were all
taken aback by the reply of one old lady, which was a long string
of Middle English curses. "Gosh, missus, where did you learn
that?", came the astonished reply.*

'Back to Frevent we marched and then began a climb into the
hills, though Nuncq and Herlin le Sec to St. Pol, a real old world
town on the River Ternoise. This was a railway junction of some
importance, for lines radiated north to Bethune, east to Arras,*

south to Frevent, Doullens and Amiens, while another line followed the river down the valley to Hesdin, Montreuil and the base areas.

'The main street of St. Pol had some beautiful house fronts, tinted with age, and life seemed to be moving peacefully with little thought of war. The busy market was typical of old France in pre-war days; countrywomen sat stolidly at their stalls knitting until some prospective buyer of butter, cheese or eggs came along.

'After passing the Gendarmerie, we turned left and marched along the valley of the Ternoise. About four kilometres on we came to Hernicourt where we went into billets. Some few lucky fellows got a bed, a luxury they had not enjoyed for nearly two years, and they made the most of it.

'In the morning the march was continued, first down the valley to Wavrans, then across the river past St. Martin's church and finally going through a lonely wooded ravine to Hestrus. Then came Tangry with a few cottages, a church and a chateau, and a kilometre further on we entered Sains-les-Pernes. Another hour's marching brought us to Fiefs, a scattered village, utterly bewildering by its many roads. The Battalion billets were naturally scattered, some being nearly ten minutes walk from HQ.

'We now looked upon this march as a tour of northern France, the chief organisers of which being the Army HQ at whose whim we marched and countermarched day after day. The whole of 31st Division. was marching north on more or less parallel roads. We rather liked being in reserve like this in spite of blistered feet and boots worn thin.

'March 23rd was spent at Fiefs as a rest day. An informal parade was held in the morning and the remainder of the day was spent more or less in a carefree manner. One man who worked hard however, was Tom Smith (Pte. 15380), the cobbler, for many boots were down to their uppers and repairs had to be done at top speed to fit men for the next day's march. A few new pairs were issued, but they were a doubtful blessing as some men found to their cost.

'Another problem was the water supply. All drinking water had to be obtained from wells. The good Curé, resembling in appearance Friar Tuck or one of Balzac's priests, lamented his village water supply, but showed us one or two wells where the *water carts could be filled. One was a deep well with slimy brick sides and a bucket and a windlass. When the bucket appeared it was full of a green jelly-like liquid that drew forth groans of dismay from the water squad. The water-cart was duly filled with 110 gallons of this watery jelly and when the right dose of chloride of lime was added it was pronounced drinkable – just about.*

'On Saturday morning, March 24th we marched off again northwards through Nedon, Amettes, Ames, Lieres, Lespesses, finally reaching the Flanders plain at Ecquedecques, a small village less than two miles from Lillers. The day's march was one of the loveliest of all the marches undertaken. The countryside was awakening to the touch of Spring, while some of the villages were almost fairylike in the beauty of the early sunshine as the morning mists unrolled. The village churches also, were worth seeing. Most of them had stood for four or five centuries and had been mellowed by the sun and rain to become almost part of the landscape.

'Here was a sane world after the horrors of the Somme. What a contrast to the smashed villages around Beaumont-Hamet, where only a signboard gave any indication that a village had once existed there, where roads were muddy quagmires, and fields were pockmarked with thousands of shell-holes, where woods and copses had been blasted into pitiable naked stumps of trees, where water became the very enemy of man, insidiously undermining every operation attempted, where death brooded over the desolate wastes.

'There was more than a physical restoration to this march. It gave us again that mental balance, unhinged by the almost intolerable conditions of trench warfare in Winter. Contact with this peaceful world made us forget the grim past, and light-heartedly we marched forward knowing that nothing could be worse than what we had already experienced.

'Sunday, 25th March was Passion Sunday and we moved off to the pealing of bells in the old church of Ecquedecques bringing to mind a parodied version of a lovely verse by F. V. Lucas:*[1]

> In Picardy the churches are cool and white and quaint,
> With here and there a crucifix, and here and there a saint
> And here and there a little shrine with candles short and tall
> That Frenchmen light for love of Him, the Lord who loveth all.

'Here were villagers in their Sunday best, going to confess their sins to some rusty-cassocked priest, or to say an 'Ave' for a son at the front.

'On we marched, through Lillers, Busnes, Robecq, along the riverside to Callonne and finally halted at Merville, a little town of about 7,000 inhabitants, at the junction of two streams with the River Lys. It was the end of the 'Long March'.

'The gods had been kind. Z Company was billeted in the town and we spent a very happy fortnight there. Big shops proved a great attraction and many a soldier's pay found it's way across the numerous counters for souvenirs to send home. To examine the varied stock before buying was a pleasure all its own. In the Grand Place was a good restaurant – (good by comparison) where every evening we enjoyed good suppers.

'Some of us wandered about the town, observing interestingly the quaint Flemish style of many of the houses, the colour-washed house fronts, the old Town Hall and other architectural features so different from those in Lancashire. The Lys Canal too, interested many, some by its possibilities for fishing, others were fascinated by the huge locks, the swing bridges and it's unusual lift (or draw) bridges.

'French lessons began in Merville – a sign in a well curtained window inviting all inside "French taught here". The teacher was not too prepossessing and soon the pupils languished, saying they could do better in the streets. There was too, the attractive, vivacious laundress posing as a widow for the duration, who washed shirts and socks to keep the wolf from the door – or so she said. She did a roaring trade.

'On Palm Sunday Merville staged a great religious procession. Black-robed priests, white-clad children with flowers in hands and hair, demure damsels in long white dresses, sturdy fellows carrying effigies of the saints, old ladies in lace caps and bonnets, all combined to make a spectacle many of us remembered for a long time. Not least impressive were the firemen and the town's band with its curious brass instruments they played with such vigour and joie de vivre.

'All good things come to an end, and on Easter Day, April 8th, we marched off again to the south, where the Vimy Ridge battle was about to begin. It was a beautiful morning with huge white clouds like sails of great galleons rolling across the sky. The men took up the hymn Christ the Lord is risen today, *singing*

The Market Place in Bethune. Typical of many towns in Northern France.
(The Taylor Library)

lustily as they marched. Memories flashed back to old grey churches in England where that same hymn was rising to high heaven.

'On we marched, through Hinges and it's big Gothic church at the cross-roads, into Bethune and out again on the south-west side, finally reaching Fonquereuil where billets were found. News came through on April 10th. that the Canadians had captured Vimy Ridge, and rumour had it that this was to be the Battalion's new battleground.*

'On Wednesday April 11th orders came to move again. This time only a short march to Houchin, just behind Noeux les Mines, but we marched along in a snowstorm and then we found the billets were tents – and there were no blankets! In this part of France two centuries ago the French had resisted the Duke of Marlborough and the English earned for themselves undying fame: "The English troops swore terribly in Flanders". They must have been exceptionally versatile to beat the English of 1917.*

'Houchin itself was the most picturesque village yet seen. It's red-roofed houses huddled together in true medieval style, with a steely blue spire topping all. It might have been taken straight out of a child's book of fairy tales.*

'The march was resumed on the 14th., through Barlin, Maisnil la Ruitz and then over the breezy hills to Ranchicourt, through La Comte to Magnicourt en Comte. Here we stayed fourteen days marching and counter-marching. On the 23rd. a grand attack on a wood at Chelers was carried out successfully – or so the umpires said.*

73

'*A continental edition of the* Daily Mail, *several days old, told of fruitless attacks in Oppy Wood. The men quickly associated their sham attacks with this wood of ill-repute – and later events proved them right.*

'*Sunday the 29th was moving day again. We marched all day through Frevillers, Bethonsart, Savy, Aubigny, Frevin Capelle, Acq, Ecoivres and Bray to Maroeuil, a dilapidated village on the River Scarpe, two or three miles from Arras. Next day the Battalion was issued with all the necessary equipment to go back into the line again. It had leaked out that the East Yorks were to attack Oppy Wood and the West Yorks were to attack at Gavrelle, while the 94 Brigade was to hold the lines near the points of attack.*

'*Our marching days were over – reality was about to set in.*'

1. Edward Verrall Lucas (1868 - 1938) – an English essayist, poet and novelist.

Following the Trail of the long March

When returning to the coast from the Serre sector of the Somme battlefields one has two choices. Firstly, there is the direct route by autoroute by way of Bapaume and junction 14 on the A1-E15, joining the A26-E15 at junction 16 near Arras and so direct to Calais and the ferry or Channel Tunnel as one wishes.

Secondly, there is a more leisurely, much less direct, but certainly more picturesque, way which will follow, in part, the Pal's 'Long March' of 18 - 25 March 1917. At St. Pol one has a choice, depending on time and inclination, to leave the Pals Trail and go to the coast via Hesdin, Montreuil and Boulogne for Calais; or continue towards Lillers and there join the A26-E15 autoroute at junction 5 and so to Calais. To complete the Pals Trail continue to Merville – some twenty kilometres beyond – this is well worth a visit.

The Long March

Pte. Crabtree's description begins: 'On Sunday 18th March the Battalion marched away from Courcelles in a westward direction...'

The present day traveller, therefore, can consider his journey starts from the same place. The following route is based on the 1995 Michelin *Carte Routiere et Touristique* No. 236, Flanders-Artois Picardy.

Start
18 March – Courcelles to Authie
D114 to Bertrancourt
D176E & D176 to Bus-les-Artois
D176 to Authie (past Warnimont Wood).
19 March – Authie to Beauval

D152 to Marieux
D11 & D31 to Beauquesne
D31 & N25 to Beauval
20 March – Beauval to Ligny-sur-Canche
N25 to Doullens (passing close to Gezaincourt)
D916 to Frevent
D941 to Ligny-sur-Canche
21 March – Ligny-sur-Canche to Hernicourt
D941 to Frevent
D916 to Nuncq
D916 to Herlin-le-Sec
D916 to St. Pol
D343 to Hernicourt
22 March – Hernicourt to Fiefs
D343 to Wavrans-sur-Ternoise
D99 to St. Martin
D99 to Hestrus
D99 to Tangry
D99 to Sains-les-Pernes
D77 to Fiefs
23 March – at Fiefs
24 March – Fiefs to Ecquedecques
D77E to Nedon
D69 to Amettes
D69 to Ames
D91 to Lieres
D91 to Lespesses
D185E to Ecquedecques
25 March – Ecquedecques to Merville
D185 to Lillers
D916 to Busnes
D94 to Robecq
D69 to Callone-sur-la-Lys
D23 to Merville
    Finish

Useful maps are:
1. Michelin Carte Routiere et Touristique
No. 236 Nord. Flandres – Artois – Picardie.
1/200000 – 1cm. : 2km.
2. Michelin Carte A
No. 51 Boulogne – Lille. 1/200000 – 1cm. : 2km.
3. As above but No. 52 Amiens.
Note: Commonwealth War Cemeteries and Memorials overprinted versions also available.
4. Cartes I.G.N. (Institute Geographique National).

a	Serie Bleue	1: 25000
b	Serie Orange	1: 50000
c	Serie Verte	1: 100000
d	Serie Rouge	1: 250000

The road from Doullens to Tangry was followed by other British troops during the Second World War. On 13 August 1944 German forces began their retreat from Normandy, where there had been ferocious fighting. 7th Armoured Division (the Desert Rats) were ordered to drive towards Ghent. On 1 September their tanks crossed the Somme at Picquigny, north west of Amiens and, driving through Domart and Berneuil, they arrived at Doullens by nightfall. The following day – observing their commanding officer's order 'Push on and don't bugger about' – the tanks of the 8th Hussars went on to Frevent. There was a sharp fight, where, with the help of French resistance fighters, eighty prisoners were taken. Speed was vital so St. Pol was bypassed because of German anti-tank guns in the town (to be dealt with by following troops) and the Hussars advanced to Tangry, where they stayed the night. The British forces carried on to capture Lillers, Bethune and Lens before entering Ghent on 5 September 1944.

Source: *Churchill's Desert Rats* by Patrick Delaforce, published by Alan Sutton 1994.

3. Sniping Irons – Fred Sayer

'An incident which shocked me, although it had its ludicrous side, happened on a nice sunny day. As I walked round a fire bay I came across a fellow rigging up a "Heath Robinson" contrivance. He was unaware that I was there and I saw a look of deep satisfaction as he surveyed his work. The scheme consisted of a heavy steel snipers plate and some wood and string which I assumed was destined to break his leg and give him a Blighty ticket.

'I spoke to him quietly. He had often confided in me and he had many troubles at home (mostly his fault). He was surprised when I spoke but immediately agreed with my suggestion that what he was doing was a bit dangerous if the wrong fellow saw him. I carried on my way. Then I returned a little later, the sniping iron was back in its place on the parapet and the bits of wood and string tossed away.

'My worrying friend was wounded in the Oppy attack and got his Blighty ticket legitimately. I met him once after the war, he was nursing another of his little troubles, a hefty boy, but sniping irons were never mentioned.'

4. Gone Missing – Fred Sayer

'On one of my trips to the field hospital, I saw some personal *equipment lying by the roadside. It was covered in mud and looked a wreck. On examination it proved to be a full set of webbing set up for 'battle-dress'. We in 31st Division had leather equipment. It dated back a bit and needed much treatment with dubbing. It was also difficult to remove mud stains. Webbing could be washed and made as new by treatment with 'blanco'. I 'rescued' my find. It added just a bit of spice to life. Something fresh.*

'Bill or "Wessy", (he came from Westmorland), was the Medical Officer's batman. He was a true countryman, aged about forty, and he loved to entertain us with romantic and tragic tales of the fells and dales. He kept the M.O. well polished and spick and span and the M.O.'s webbing was perfect. As Wessy was one of our bunch, he naturally got busy with my find and it was soon up to the M.O.'s standard.

'I had hardly worn it when Wessy's leave came through. We were all delighted and everyone helped to make him smart and happy. He looked on top of the world in my new webbing, with the haversack full of our contributions of cigarettes, chocolate, etc. and I wondered if my own leave would come through before he returned.

'Easy come! Easy go! That was the last I saw of my smart outfit. Wessy got to Blighty alright, but we never heard of him again. He drifted, to put it kindly. We often debated where he could be. We guessed he grew a beard and became a shepherd away in those fells and dales in the "Lakes", where he probably did more good than tending our M.O.'

5. Food – Fred Sayer

'In addition to all our troubles we had undernourished bodies. I had a remarkable mother and we were a family of eight children. "If you buy the best food, you will not spend money on doctor's bills", was mother's frequent remark. We all enjoyed her food and her joke. Army food, however, after her glorious breads and pastries, left the imagination agog for a reunion.

'Bread in the form of a round cottage loaf, without the top hit, came from army bakehouses at the base. It was good bread, but white. Wholemeal would have been better for our health. The loaves were carried in huge sacks and suffered somewhat in transit. To get them to the trenches they had to be carried in sandbags. The latter had an oily smell. Bread needs to smell of

yeast. By the time we got the bread in the line (if we got it) the loaves could be damp, wet, muddy, oily, just lumps of dough or just crushed. Of course when the bread was missing, there were army biscuits. These were wholemeal and wholesome. They could be soaked for a day or so and made into a pudding with tinned milk and jam. In the trenches one just gnawed them, as did the rats, who I guess, got more of the biscuits than the troops.

'*Meat came to units deep frozen, and in winter this is where the cooks got their daily exercise. Bashing a side of beef, and it was good beef, needed tree-felling axes. The field kitchens could fry or boil, so we got boiled frozen meat. It was not practical to make a palatable dish, even a stew, by cooking lumps of frozen beef, even if you were a professional. Our cooks were not, they were of various trades. In fact, the sergeant in charge was an umbrella salesman.*

'*Bacon was probably the most welcome meal, depending whether the issue, which came in sides, had been washed, and or, soaked. Otherwise it was very salty. It was quite a problem for the cooks who had to slice it by hand.*

'*Cheese was one of the chief protein foods. It was usually well-matured and hard. It was quite versatile and practicable. It could be carried in the pocket, nibbled at and scraped or washed if dirty. Quite sociable.*

'*Corned beef was the mainstay in the line. One make from the U.S.A. had jelly instead of fat, but generally the fat was left on*

Troops enjoying a welcome meal.

the meat. This made it too rich to be eaten without vegetables. One day we were asked if we would like beans. After eating 'bully' for six months, naturally we agreed – anything for a change. We got nothing but beans after that for over a month and were glad if we found a tin of bully that may have been trampled on or blown into the mud.

'Vegetables were limited to dried mixed anything and were put into stews. They were not a success as the cooks could not give them the required soaking. The lack of fruit and particularly vegetables affected the life of everyone. Even out of the line it was rarely possible to get any. The only greens I recollect having in 1917 was when I was in a garden behind the line where there were some sprouts. I just ate some raw, turning my back on the owner, who would not sell us any.

'Drinks consisted of tea and water. The latter was heavily chlorinated and had, of course, to be carried up to the line like the rest of the rations. The tea was made in the dixies that cooked the stew and drunk from the canteens from which the stew had been eaten. In the dark if you called it soup, it tasted like soup. If it was warm it was very welcome and if it was hot, it was a miracle.'

6. Aspirins – Fred Sayer

'In the line I began to get angry that there was no treatment for sick men. Aspirins would have been invaluable. This drug had been available in Blighty in the form of flakes (almost like soap flakes) which we called 'Soda Sal' (acetylsalicylic acid). It had been invented in Germany and came to England before the war. Dr. Hodges in Burnley thought the world of it and I must have dispensed thousands of bottles of the stuff mixed with various essences as a tonic. Here we were with scores of fever cases and no aspirins, although they were now made in tablet form.

'When we got out of the line, I asked the M.O. for a "chit" addressed to the M.O. of the Field Hospital in the form of a requisition for a hundred aspirins. It was an eight mile walk – there and back. The sergeant in charge of medical supplies nearly blasted me out of the hut when I showed him my chit. I told him "It is not addressed to you but to your M.O. and if you don't like it, I'll go to see him"

'I was wearing a huge sheep-skin coat, the lower part of

79

which was well matted with trench mud. The sergeant looked me over, but did not ask my rank. Suddenly, he produced a bottle of aspirins tipped out a handful and said "Will that satisfy you?" . I counted them until there was one hundred, then counted them again – ninety nine – for I had taken one whilst he was not looking at me.

'Feeling a real filibuster, I was as near to dancing as I would ever be in my big muddy boots, at the successful manoeuvre. I just hugged those tablets. Of course, it might have been the aspirin filched that created the light–headedness, but I certainly felt better.

'Our supply of the tablets was quickly used as there was quite a demand. With mild attacks of Trench Fever they did the job and most people were able to shrug off the attack after a couple of days rest.

'I got another chit, hoping someone else would be in charge at the hospital when I arrived. At the hospital I told them we had an epidemic of fever and they could expect up to fifty cases in the next few days. "With aspirins who knows?" "Please come and see". I had no trouble getting aspirins after that. I always counted them and the number was always short. They were wily counters at that hospital.'

Shortly after this Fred Sayer went on home leave. He then spent five months in a military hospital near Whalley, a few miles from his home in Burnley. On his recovery he was posted to 3 (Reserve) Battalion, East Lancashire Regiment, at Saltburn, Yorkshire, North Riding. He volunteered to return to France and was attached to 84 Company, Chinese Labour Corps. He served with them as a medical orderly until the Armistice.

7. Operations at Oppy – Failure – May 1917

On May Day 1917, 31st Division relieved 63rd (Royal Naval) Division on the Gavrelle – Oppy sector of the line north of Arras. 92 Brigade took over the right sub-sector (Gavrelle) with 93 Bgde. in the left (Oppy). The Battalion was in support of 93 Bgde. They assembled in old German trenches behind the ruined village of Bailleul. This was the apex of a triangle with Oppy and Gavrelle at the other corners.

From the beginning it was an unhappy time for the Battalion. After dark on 3 May the Battalion took over the line in front of Oppy. Immediately there began a hectic night throwing bombs into the

Above: Oppy village and wood taken before the battle commenced. Right: This photograph shows the village and wood on April 30, 1917. Though some of the buildings still stand, all have been damaged.

View of Oppy from the approximate position of Wood Alley Trench. *(The Pals Collectio...)*

German trenches. These were simply a continuation of the British trench and an old German communication trench. Only piles of sandbags and coils of barbed wire separated the opposing troops and there was much ferocious bombing between the two. All the while, German shells pounded the line.

On 5 May the Battalion was relieved and moved into old German dug-outs in the railway cutting near Bailleul. The dug-outs were huge places, holding hundreds of men. Wire beds ran alongside the walls in two or three tiers, but the doorways faced the front line and the German shellfire. Fortunately, there were few casualties.

On 7 May the Battalion went back into the line. The daylight hours were fairly quiet but each night there were constant bombing raids by the enemy, preceded by heavy shellfire. These raids caused the deaths of two officers and six men and wounded thirty-three men. It was a welcome relief to move back to the railway cutting on 9 May.

The Battalion returned to the line on the evening of 12 May. Almost

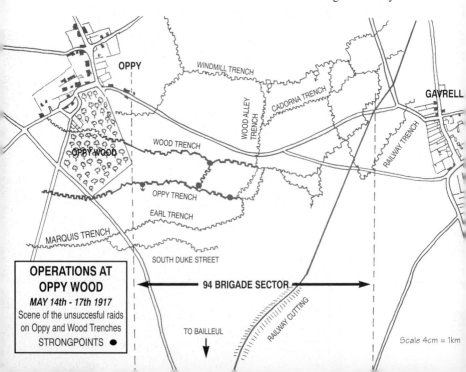

immediately the enemy attempted to raid the trenches but were driven back by rifle and machine gun fire.

On the night of 13/14 May a bombing party, led by 2/Lt. Lott, with support from trench mortar and rifle grenade fire, attacked a strongpoint in Oppy Trench, south of the village. Several attempts to break through the wire around the strongpoint were unsuccessful and the party retired.

The following night, 15 May, two parties attacked. One, under 2/Lt. Lott, worked up Oppy Trench. The other, under 2/Lt. McKenzie, up Wood Trench. Both were supported by trench mortar and rifle grenade fire. Both parties reached the trench connecting Oppy and Wood Trenches, but found it full of wire. The enemy was by then on both flanks and a bombing duel went on for some twenty minutes before both parties returned to a strongpoint just north of Railway Trench. Even here the bombing parties were not secure. At 5.30 am the enemy counter-attacked and took the strongpoint. It was soon recovered, but this second attack had already failed.

On the night of 16/17 May, after a bombardment by British heavy artillery, a third attempt was made to capture the strong-point in Oppy Trench. The enemy were waiting. They threw bombs on the two parties immediately they moved forward. A machine gun also opened fire from a position behind the enemy post. After fifteen minutes of heavy bombing from both flanks it was evident the enemy were fully prepared for any attack. Moreover, the mud and the darkness prevented

A bombing raid on German postions at Oppy. An artists impression. *(The Pals Collection)*

any rapid movement. It was decided to break off the attack – a third failure.

On the night of 19 May the Battalion was relieved and they moved to the railway cutting near Bailleul. Casualties amounted to three officers and thirteen men killed and thirty-six men wounded, with one man missing.

On 20 May, 63rd (Royal Naval) Division took over from 31st Division. For the Battalion at least it had been a most unhappy and unsuccessful tour of the line. The Battalion did not, as expected, go back to their old billets at Roclincourt but, marching through Thelus and Neuville St. Vaast, went to Mont St. Eloi.

Here the men received some pay. L/Cpl. Crabtree, no less than the others, was pleased as well as relieved. 'Here were some good hutments and some villages where money could be spent.'

The officers and men who died are buried in a number of cemeteries. Three are commemorated on the Arras Memorial. Two officers and ten men are buried in Albuhera Cemetery, Bailleul. 2/Lt. Errol William Leach lies in Orchard Dump Cemetery, Arluex-en-Gohelle. He was buried there after the Armistice when the cemetery was enlarged by the concentration of remains from battlefield graves. Of the ten who died of wounds, four are in Duisans British Cemetery, Etrun. Three lie in Ste. Catherine British Cemetery, Anzin St. Aubin. Two men died of wounds in hospital at Etaples and are buried in Etaples Military Cemetery. 26961 L/Cpl. James Ward, previously reported missing, died as a prisoner of war. He was buried by the Germans and his body removed to Douai British Cemetery after the Armistice.

7. Operations at Oppy – Success – May 1917

On 10 June, 31st Division relieved 63rd (Royal Naval) Division in the Gavrelle – Oppy sector. The Battalion, in turn, relieved Hawke Battalion in the Oppy sub-sector.

The Battalion spent the next nine days observing and probing the enemy lines. It was a 'quiet' time, without incident, and most men dug assembly and forward communication trenches in readiness for the attack planned for 28 June.

On the night of 19 June they were relieved by 13 York and Lancaster Regiment and then marched to Ecurie. Here they rehearsed for the coming attack. On 23 June they took part in a full scale Brigade rehearsal at Maroeuil. The object of 31st Division's attack was firstly to maintain pressure on the Arras front and secondly, to divert the

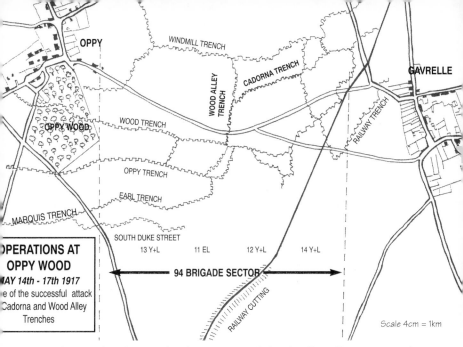

enemy's attention from a simultaneous attack by the Canadians near
Lens, to the north. The local objective was to remove the small salient,
full of machine gun strongpoints, which had been the scene of the
failed attacks in May.

The Battalion's role was to take the northern part of Cadorna Trench
plus Wood Alley to its junction with the Oppy to Gavrelle road. (Wood
Trench and Oppy Trench, scene of the operations in May, were to the
Battalion's left, to be attacked by 13 York and Lancaster Regiment).
The Battalion moved into the line on 26 June. The Germans suspected

The remains of Oppy Wood in 1917.

an attack and shelled the incoming troops, causing several casualties. On 27 June several British shells fell short onto Z Company, causing more casualties. 28 June dawned warm but cloudy and the men had an anxious wait, under intermittent shell fire, until Zero hour – set at 7.10 pm.

Lt Wilton, X Company commander, was wounded at this time so Major Kershaw, temporarily in command of the Battalion in the absence of Lieutenant Colonel Rickman, who was at Brigade Headquarters, asked 2/Lt Lott to take his place.

When Zero Hour at last arrived, the British artillery opened fire with a brief but ferocious barrage onto the German front line. Simultaneously, the Battalion assault companies (W, X and Z, with Y in support) moved quickly across No Man's Land, and with few casualties, took Cadorna Trench. The advance took just over eight minutes. Many of the defending troops were bayoneted and others shot by Lewis guns in hand to hand fighting.

2/Lt. Wheeldon of W Company and Sergeant Southworth, his platoon sergeant, were the first to reach the enemy trenches. 2/Lt Wheeldon was met by four Germans, who he killed single-handed although he was wounded in both arms and legs by a bomb thrown by one of the four. In a melee of hand to hand fighting, Sergeant Southworth killed three more of the enemy. The rest of them surrendered. Sergeant Southworth then took command of the remainder of the platoon and led them in consolidating their position. 2/Lt Lott meanwhile, led X Company with 'great dash and ability' to their objective. During his consolidation of the position he disregarded all danger whilst moving about in the open encouraging his men.

When Z Company reached their objective 2/Lt Lonsdale also organised their consolidation with great courage and determination until he was compelled to give in to the effects of a wound to his arm. The three companies stayed in their respective positions and all speedily dealt with enemy counter attacks. Immediately the positions were captured, Lewis gun teams went forward across the macadamised Oppy to Gavrelle road to cover the consolidation. The Battalion stayed in the captured trenches during 29 June, by which time the Germans had recovered sufficiently to bring heavy artillery fire on the new British front line. This, causing mounting casualties, continued until 1 July.

L/Cpl Crabtree worked in an Aid Post. His description gives a glimpse of conditions there:

'The Aid Post was a slit about eight yards long, off the main

A casualty being treated at a Regimental Aid Post.

communication trench and just behind the front line. We became the target for the German gunners. The only protection was a sheet of corrugated iron to keep out the rain. In one hour over fifty shells dropped around this shelter and never hit the trench, though every few minutes a shower of mud, clay and splinters fell like hail on the tin roof. Four stretcher cases were in the shelter and two more were in the trench outside while several walking wounded crouched under what little cover they could get and roundly cursed their unhappy situation. In the short intervals in the shelling the [Z] Company stretcher bearers brought in more wounded. These we dressed quickly and R.A.M.C. bearers took them to the rear.'

On the night of 1/2 July the Battalion was relieved and went to Ecurie in reserve. On 3 July they marched to Maroeuil and were billeted in

Oppy Wood and the village from the site of the Regimental Aid Post.
(The Pals Collection)

tents. A ten day 'rest and reorganisation' period followed. L/Cpl. Crabtree recalled:'New gas respirators were issued and were tested in special gas chambers. They certainly were an improvement on the old clammy bag that fitted over the head like a Ku Klux Klan head-dress'.

The human cost of the Battalion's success was twelve men killed and four officers and ninety-two men wounded. At least two men died of their wounds. None of the dead were either recovered or later identified so their names are on the Arras Memorial. The two men wounded lie in Duisans British Cemetery, Etrun, near their comrades from the May bombing raids.

Major John Victor Kershaw was the initiator and planner of the Battalion attack. Its success gained him the award of the Distinguished Service Order. 2/Lt Frederick Lawrence Wheeldon was also awarded the DSO. For his part of the same action Sergeant Thomas Southworth received the Distinguished Conduct Medal. 2/Lt William Farrer

Lonsdale's 'pluck and determination' won him the Military Cross. 2/Lt John Cyprian Lott's award of the Military Cross for his 'splendid example of coolness and disregard for danger', also took into account his leadership and gallantry when leading the three bombing raids at Oppy in May. Sadly, 2/Lt Lott was killed in action near Vieux Berquin on 13 April 1918. He is buried in Outtersteene Communal Cemetery Extension, Bailleul. His body was re-interred there from a battlefield grave after the Armistice.

88

Sgt T Southworth.
(The Pals Collection)

CHAPTER FOUR

An Eventful Year:
January 1918 - December 1918

1. Dawn in a Quiet Sector, – Percy Crabtree

'*The night passed quietly. Men not on immediate duty soon got down in tiny cubby holes to try to sleep. Sentries peered over the decrepit sandbags, trying to disentangle tree stumps from the enveloping darkness, and generally becoming convinced that someone was stealthily making his way to the trench to throw in a bomb.*

'*"Bill, come here and have a look". "There's something moving over there, by that shell hole – if it is a shell hole". Bill climbed on the firestep. "Can't see owt" said he. Just then the platoon sergeant came round the traverse, calling, "Patrol out – should be back by two o'clock – careful, you chaps." The sentry, easier in mind now, turned to his companion and with withering scorn almost shouted, "I told you so; I knew there was somebody moving out there", pointing with his thumb into no man's land.*

'*So the night passed. Patrols and wiring parties came in, the men throwing themselves down anywhere to drop off to sleep immediately. Sentries were relieved and the interminable watching continued.*

'*The eastern sky turned from black to grey, stars grew feeble and became lost in the lightening dawn. "Stand to! Stand to!" resounded along the trench. Sleepy men stumbled to their feet. Dugouts emptied of their men and soon all turned east to face any assault likely to be launched against them. It seemed like some solemn rite of sun-worshippers, who at the first glimpse of the red ball appearing on the horizon, stood armed and silent in the presence of their God.*

'Peaceful and majestic came the dawn. Soon the order 'Stand down' relieved the men straining their eyes to the east. The rum ration was issued, giving an artificial gaiety and a certain physical warmth to counteract the chill of the early morning.

'Breakfast preparations proceeded apace. Tommy cookers appeared. Shredded sandbags and small slices of candle ignited between two bricks made a capital fire on which to boil a dixie tin of tea. Tins of pork and beans or bully beef were opened. Bread that morning was a loaf to five men but there were biscuits to eke out!

'Diminutive curls of smoke like incense came from both British and German lines and half an hour's peace followed; the men growing more talkative as the sun rose higher and sent some warmth into the trench.

'The day's activities began. Sandbags were filled and carefully placed in weak spots in the breastwork; duckboards were replaced; sump holes were covered up; telephone wires were pinned back into the trench walls and scores of other small jobs were done.

'A stretcher bearer going down the trench, seeing a sentry peering over the top of the sandbags, said "Use a periscope, he has a machine gun fixed on this bay" . "Nowt at sort" came the reply, "Besides, I can't see owt with this blasted thing".

'"Never mind old chap, keep your head down and your hair on," answered the stretcher bearer.

'The stretcher bearer, returning some minutes later, noticed the queer posture of the sentry. He was leaning against the side of the bay, his rifle having slid on to the duckboards. Angry at the man's carelessness after warning him of the danger, the stretcher bearer asked somewhat impatiently where he was hit.

'No answer came save a shuddering moan. Then, as the wounded man was gently lowered to the trench floor his steel helmet fell off, showing the top of his skull grooved out, as if a V shaped chisel had done it.'

2. Action at Ayette – March, 1918

On 4 March 1918 the Battalion marched from Springvale Camp near Arras, to billets in the villages of Marquay and Bailleul-aux-Cornailles, just north of the Arras to St. Pol road. Here they settled down for 'rest and recreation', but with further training in musketry and bombing and regular route marches.

90

For L/Cpl. Percy Crabtree it was a pleasant interlude, and as always, he found time to appreciate the finer things of life.

> *'Occasionally we got a chit to visit St. Pol, a delightful old town with seventeenth century houses in the Grande Place. The beautiful colouring of the old houses and the old church delighted the artistic fellows in the Company. After the aesthetic came the material in the form of steak and chips for tea – a good preparation for the six kilometres (almost four miles) walk to Marquay along the beautiful tree-lined road through Roellecourt.'*

As the days passed the Battalion paraded, trained and marched itself into fighting trim again. In the 31st Division Football Cup competition the Battalion team beat the East Yorkshire Regiment 4-0. In the semi-final, they beat 31st Division Ambulance team 3-0, but on 21 March, in the final at Tingues, they lost to the 31st Division Ammunition Column.

Strange rumours, however, were going about. Cookhouse gossip told of Germans massing for a great attack, but to the rank and file things looked much as usual and so little attention was paid.

On Thursday 21 March, Lieutenant Colonel Rickman, after a temporary absence, returned and took command. On the same day, as the Battalion was losing in the Cup final, the Germans poured through the British front lines and reserves along a fifty mile front from Arras to La Fere. In the early morning their artillery pounded the British trenches for some five hours. Behind the barrage came hordes of specially trained assault troops, catching the British by surprise and penetrating the line in many places. They very quickly over-ran the British positions. 31st Division was ordered to move to the area to help fill the gaps and stem the breakthrough.

No one in the Battalion was surprised when reveille was at 4 a.m. on 22 March. After a hasty breakfast they boarded a fleet of buses which rushed them to Bailleulval on the south side of the Arras to Doullens road. At eleven p.m. they marched to a position east of Boisleux St. Marc. In the darkness there was hideous confusion as thousands of troops milled about.

The Battalion transport section, after a forced march of twenty-two hours, tried to find the Battalion. In the mass of men and chaos it was not easy. Nor was help always forthcoming. L/Cpl. Crabtree relates:

> *'Then came a battalion of Guards – surely no-one could mistake the steady, long, stride of these men. One Pal, remembering that 4th. Guards Brigade were part of 31st*

Division, called out "Who are you?". The troops moved in the darkness like a line of phantoms, but a voice cried out "The Guards", the sound almost lost in the rythmic din of marching feet. Not satisfied with the reply, the Pal shouted "Which Guards?". A sepulchral voice from the passing ranks superciliously said, "There's only one Guards" and the men passed on into the night.' [From this reply they could have been Grenadier Guards, the senior regiment of Foot Guards].

The Battalion, in the meantime, on arrival at Boisleux St. Marc, found their positions already taken up by the 3rd. Battalion Coldstream Guards. Because of this mistaken order, it was six a.m. before another position, astride the railway line west of Boisleux St. Marc railway station was taken up. (see 1 on sketch map page 95).

At 9-15 p.m. on 23 March, 92 Brigade, of which the Battalion was part, (together with the 10th and 11th. Battalions, East Yorkshire

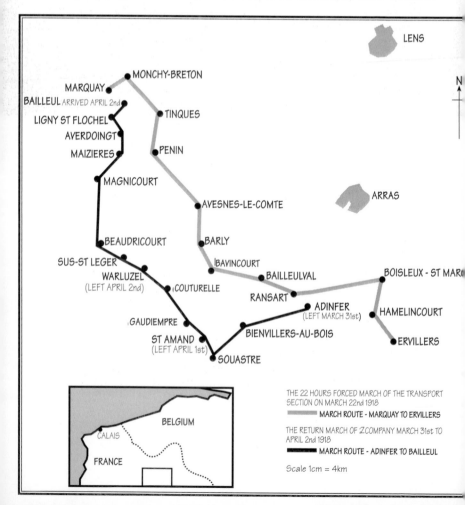

THE 22 HOURS FORCED MARCH OF THE TRANSPORT SECTION ON MARCH 22nd 1918
MARCH ROUTE - MARQUAY TO ERVILLERS

THE RETURN MARCH OF 'Z' COMPANY MARCH 31st TO APRIL 2nd 1918
MARCH ROUTE - ADINFER TO BAILLEUL

Scale 1cm = 4km

British troops on the way to meet the German offensive.

Regiment) was ordered to new positions, a defensive flank, in Divisional reserve, near Ervillers.

By one am on 24 March two companies (HQ and X) were in positions on the Gomiecourt to Hamelincourt road. W, Y and Z companies were forward on the Ervillers to Hamelincourt road. (2). It became known that troops of the hard-pressed 40th. Division on the right of the 31st Division, were due to be relieved during the night of 23/24 March, but desperately heavy fighting in the area meant that it was not known whether the relief would take place. Therefore, at 4 a.m., anxiety for the safety of the right flank caused 92 Brigade commander to send Y and X Companies to the Yellow Line in front of the railway line due east of Courcelles-le-Comte.

The day saw bitter fighting as the Brigade was heavily attacked by infantry supported by trench mortar batteries. All the attacks were beaten off, but the village of Mory, south of Ervillers, fell into German hands. This left 31st Division's flank exposed as the Germans advanced into Ervillers later in the day.

The ruins of a farmhouse in Ayette.

Monday 25 March was a critical day. At 5 p.m. the Germans were reported (incorrectly as it turned out) in Gomiecourt. The report caused the Battalion to withdraw to a position astride the railway line south of Courcelles-le-Comte. (3).

The two companies on the Yellow Line moved to the threatened flank. Battalion HQ was on the aerodrome some 800 yards east of Ayette on the Courcelles-le-Comte road. In spite of heavy shelling over open ground the positions were reached with only slight casualties. Two enemy attacks were driven off. Night fell with two companies back holding the Yellow Line and two companies anxiously watching the threatened flank.

At 4 am on 26 March enemy advances to the south made the Yellow

The Battalion positions on the Ablainzeville to Moyenneville road where it crossed the Ayette to Courcelles-le-Comte road. See (4) on map above.

To AYETTE

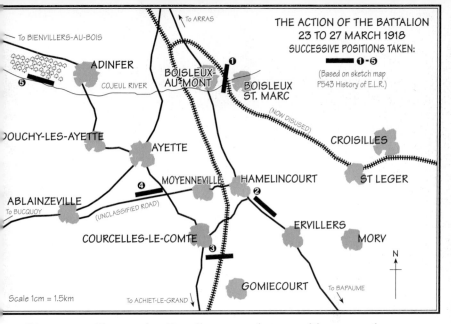

THE ACTION OF THE BATTALION
23 TO 27 MARCH 1918
SUCCESSIVE POSITIONS TAKEN:

❶-❺

(Based on sketch map
P543 History of E.L.R.)

To ARRAS

To BIENVILLERS-AU-BOIS

ADINFER

BOISLEUX-
AU-MONT

BOISLEUX
ST. MARC

COJEUL RIVER

(NOW DISUSED)

DOUCHY-LES-AYETTE

CROISILLES

AYETTE

ST LEGER

MOYENNEVILLE

HAMELINCOURT

ABLAINZEVILLE

To BUCQUOY

(UNCLASSIFIED ROAD)

ERVILLERS

MORV

COURCELLES-LE-COMTE

N

GOMIECOURT

To BAPAUME

Scale 1cm = 1.5km

To ACHIET-LE-GRAND

Line untenable so the Battalion moved to positions on the Ablainzeville to Moyenneville road where it crossed the Ayette to Courcelles-le-Comte road. (4) At 10.40 a.m. the enemy were seen in Courcelles-le-Comte. In the afternoon, they were in Moyenneville. At 11-20 a.m. on 27 March, the Germans, after a furious artillery barrage, made a frontal attack on the Battalion positions. The battalion on the left gave ground but a counter-attack at twelve noon restored the line. The enemy repeated the attack, again ground was given, and again it was restored, and the Battalion grimly held on to its position. At 12.20 p.m. the enemy made a fresh assault and although there were many casualties, 'not an inch of ground' was given and the attack repulsed. The Battalion fought doggedly all day and again contact with the units to the south was lost and the flank exposed. At 2 p.m. X Company reported 'Am still holding on to top of ridge but have very few men left. Enemy on ridge 60 yards from our position'. By now, all communication with Brigade HQ was lost.

To MOYENNEVILLE →

ADINFER WOOD

The Battalion retired, in good order, to Adinfer Wood. See (5) on map on page 95. *(The Pals Collection)*

By 4.25 pm the Germans established strong-points on the Ayette to Courcelles-le-Comte road and had come round both flanks and within 500 yards to the rear of Battalion HQ. The Battalion was therefore forced to retire to high ground south east of Ayette to a defensive line constructed overnight by the 4th Battalion, Coldstream Guards. Lieutenant Colonel Rickman then noticed the 11th. Battalion, East Yorkshire Regiment had moved further back than was intended so exposing the Battalion's flank. He gave the order to retire, in good order, to Adinfer Wood, beyond the Cojeul river. (5).

The Battalion was not engaged again after the withdrawal to Adinfer Wood. The German offensive had been effectively halted by the heroic stand of all units of 31st Division. The German troops were driven back time after time.

L/Cpl Crabtree (who had worked as a stretcher-bearer throughout, but described very little of what he did), commented,

'The Battalion was worn out. The men dazed by continuous fighting. Some could hardly stand for sheer exhaustion, but it was a glad sight to our weary, bloodshot, eyes to see the enemy retiring to the north east.'

The Battalion was relieved by the 1st. Dorset Regiment of 32nd Division, and in the early hours of Easter Sunday, 31 March, left Adinfer Wood.

'We staggered rather than marched into Bienvillers-au-Bois, to Souastre, to St. Amand, where we slept like the dead. Next morning a longer march took us through villages such Gaudiempre, where a rickety windmill lazily turned its sails.

ADINFER VILLAGE

Then we were across the Arras to Doullens road to Couturelle with its fine chateau. Finally, by way of Warluzel, to Sus St. Leger and good billets. There was little singing, for our ranks were depleted. Many had lost friends, but deep down in our hearts we all felt a great pride at the outcome of our last battle.'

The cost was high. The Battalion War Diary noted: Four officers killed and seven wounded, and a total of 339 O.R.s killed, wounded and missing. Of the dead, sixty-six with no known grave are commemorated on the Arras Memorial. Eight others died shortly afterwards, either in British or German hospitals.

In a tribute to their courage, the Battalion received a total of twenty-eight awards: One Victoria Cross; two Distinguished Service Orders; one bar to the DSO. (Lt. Col. Rickman); seven Military Crosses; three Distinguished Conduct Medals and fourteen Military Medals.

THE AERODROME AT AYETTE

R.F.C./R.A.F. records do not actually list an aerodrome for Ayette. It is listed for Courcelles-le-Comte, some four kilometres (2.5 miles) from Ayette. R.F.C. Squadrons 12, 15 and 59 operated from here during 1917, before the aerodrome

IN LOVING MEMORY
of

PRIVATE

John Willie Thomason,

11th East Lancashire Regiment,

Died of wounds received in Action, on the 28th March, 1918, at the 12th Stationary Hospital, St. Pol, France,

in his 22nd year.

We think we see his smiling face
As he bade us his last good-bye,
When he left our home for ever,
In some foreign land to die.

Yes, he's gone and how we miss him,
No one in this world can tell,
But we hope again to meet him,
Where we'll never say farewell.

Thy Will be Done.

From his sorrowing Sisters,
Brother, & Grandparents,
24, James Street,
Great Harwood,
and Father, in Dover.

(The Pals Collection)

was abandoned in March 1918 in the face of the German advance.

There is now no trace of the 'drome. The most likely site is an area approximately 1.25 kilometres (three-quarters of a mile) east of Ayette on the Courcelles-le-Comte road: (The Battalion War Diary says it is 800 yards.) The Ayette Indian and Chinese Cemetery lies between the supposed site and the village.

As one travels towards Ayette from Courcelles-le-Comte the crest of the ridge on which the Ablainzeville to Moyenneville road crosses, can be seen. The area of relatively flat land just beyond is the likely site of the aerodrome.

2/Lt. Horsfall's defence line was on the ridge, therefore, when he and his men retired towards Ayette and Adinfer Wood, they would cross the 'drome.

A valuable map reference is the I.G.N., France, 1:25000 (4cm.-1km) map 24 07 Est (Bapaume est).

2/Lt. BASIL ARTHUR HORSFALL V.C.

(The Pals Collection)

The Pal's only Victoria Cross was won by 2/Lt. B.A. Horsfall in an extraordinary example of courage and tenacity and disregard for danger, on 27 March 1918, near the village of Ayette.

Basil Arthur Horsfall was the youngest of the four sons of Mr. W.F. Horsfall of Columbo, Ceylon (now Sri Lanka). He was born on 4 October 1887 and, at the age of fifteen, entered the Sir William Borlase's School, Marlow, Berkshire. In addition to his academic skills he was an outstanding sportsman, playing both cricket and football for the school. In 1905, his final year, he was Captain of the School.

He returned to Columbo and entered the Public Works Department as an Accountant. In August 1912 he was an Assistant Accountant and Storekeeper and in April 1914 was appointed a Financial Assistant and Accountant. When war broke out he at once applied for leave to England to enlist, this was refused as the Ceylon Engineer Volunteers, of which he was a member, was at that time, on work of national importance to Ceylon.

On 11 July 1916, however, after finally receiving permission, he left Ceylon for England. He was gazetted to The East Lancashire Regiment on 19 December 1916. He went to France in February 1917 and served with the 1st. Battalion (his brother E. F. Horsfall, was his company commander) until he was wounded in an attack on the Chemical Works at Rouex, near Arras, in May. Although wounded himself, when he knew his brother and another officer were also wounded, he took command of the company. Although fainting from loss of blood, it was

98

five hours before he agreed to go to a dressing station. He went to hospital in England and returned, transferred to the Pals, on 24 October 1917.

On 27 March 1918, during the German offensive, the Pals were under very heavy attack by German forces in their attempts to capture Ayette. (see pages 94-96). The Germans stormed the Pal's positions astride the Courcelles-le-Comte to Ayette road again and again, with each side suffering heavy losses. 2/Lt. Horsfall was in command of the centre company and held the ridge along which ran the road from Ablainzeville to Moyenneville. It was the key to the Battalion's position.

During the attacks 2/Lt Horsfall's forward sections were driven back and he himself was wounded in the head. In spite of his wound he re-organised the remainder of his men and attacked and recovered the original position. He was then told that two of his three officers (2/Lt's Gardner and Hollinshead) were killed and the other wounded. Because of this, he refused, in spite of his severe wound, to go to a dressing station. Again he and his men withdrew because of heavy shell-fire and again he ordered a counter-attack which regained the position. Later in the day Lieutenant Colonel Rickman ordered the Battalion to retire in good order to Adinfer Wood. When 2/Lt. Horsfall received the order he was the last to leave the position and although exhausted, said he could have held on if necessary.

The citation in the *London Gazette* dated 23 May 1918 for the award of the Victoria Cross stated it was 'for most conspicuous bravery and devotion to duty'. The citation ended 'His conduct was a splendid example to his men and he showed throughout the utmost disregard for danger. This very gallant officer was killed when returning to the positions to the rear'.

In 1985 ex-Pte. Arthur Cheetham described a little of what happened.

(The Pals Collection)

> *'The order to retire came. Before we set off our C.O. shouted 'Every man for himself!' Terrible words to hear, but it was a terrible situation to be in. Lt Horsfall was on my left as we started to cross the aerodrome at Ayette. After twenty yards or so, I looked to my left and he simply wasn't there. Our company lost about twenty-five men crossing that aerodrome. There were five of us in our party and two did not make it. I made two crossings that day so I consider I was very lucky. Of all the time I spent in France that was a day I will never forget.'*

Mr. Cheetham died in 1989. About two years before, he had his first

ever X-ray. Unknown to him, there was a bullet lodged in his chest. It was decided to leave it where it had been for almost seventy years.

2/Lt. Horsfall's body was never found. Neither were the bodies of 2/Lt. Sydney Gardner and 2/Lt. Shadrach Hollinshead. All three are commemorated on the Arras Memorial, together with another officer, 2/Lt. Albert Bell.

2/Lt. Horsfall is remembered by his old school. His name is on the war memorial in the school chapel and a framed photograph of him was presented to the school by his brother, C.W. Horsfall, in October 1958.

Following the Battlefield Trail

Day one of the battle – 23 March, 1918
From Boisleux St. Marc, take the D35 to Boisleux-au-Mont, then the D36 to Hamelincourt and continue to Ervillers.
24 March
There is no direct road from Gomiecourt to Hamelincourt. Firstly, take the unclassified road onto the D9E, near the railway bridge. At the next junction by the railway line, bear right onto the D12. Turn left into Hamelincourt at the junction with the D36.
25 March
'Astride the railway line south of Courcelles-le-Comte' (From the War Diary) This position was probably in the area of the present Warry Copse Cemetery (F619). (The cemetery is accessible from the D9E, Ervillers to Courcelles-le-Comte road).
26 March
The road from Courcelles-le-Comte to Ayette is unclassified. Also unclassified is the road from Ablainzeville to Moyenneville. This crosses the Courcelles-le-Comte to Ayette road at a point known as Vallee d' Abbesse.
27 March
The move to Adinfer Wood. Through Ayette on D919 for a short distance in village, then turn right onto D7 to Douchy-les-Ayette. Continue on D7 to Adinfer. Adinfer Wood (Bois d'Adinfer) is to the left.
31 March
The march to the rear from Adinfer Wood. Take the D35 from Adinfer to Monchy-au-Bois, then the D2 to Bienvillers-au-Bois. Continue on the D2 to Souastre then turn right onto the D23 to

Couterelle in 1998. *The Pals Collection*

St. Amand – 'where we slept like the dead' (Percy Crabtree).
1 April
From St. Amand to Gaudiempre on D23. Continue on the D23 to Couturelle (crossing the N25 Arras to Doullens road). Continue on D23 through Warluzel to Sus-St. Leger.

The most suitable maps to use are:
General map: Michelin No.2 36 Nord 1: 200000
Local maps: I.G.N. France 24.07 Bapaume est 1:25000
               I.G.N. France 24.07 Bapaume ouest 1:25000

3. Battle of the Lys – April, 1918

The Battalion was still re-organising and training at Bailleul-aux-Cornailles when the second German attempt to break through the British front line was launched. At 4.15 am on 9 April the German army mounted an offensive between Armentieres in the north and the La Bassee Canal in the south. The main force of the attack fell on the line near Neuve Chapelle on the River Lys, but such was the force of the storm that by nightfall on 10 April German troops were not only in Armentieres, some two miles (3 kms.) behind the British lines, but also in Steenwerke and Estaires.

L/Cpl Crabtree and his colleagues heard the news in the evening of 9 April,

> *'We're for it again', lamented one fellow, remembering Ayette. He was promptly shut up by his pal saying, 'Never mind, old chap, we've stopped him once, and we'll do it again'.*

31st Division was rushed to the north in buses to the new point of

Le Paradis on the D947 looking towards Stazeele station in 1998.

The Pals Collection

danger. The Battalion moved in the darkness and arrived at Le Paradis, on the Vieux Berquin to Strazeele road on 11 April. Patrols pushed forward to Bleu, a tiny cluster of cottages, east of Vieux Berquin.

In the confusion and noise of gunfire from both sides L/Cpl. Crabtree became involved in his own rescue mission:

> *'That night a moated farm was struck by shells and blazed furiously. Screams came from the doomed building and we rushed in to rescue a woman and her child. Cattle, maddened by the crashing shells, dashed about in terror. We rounded them up and slapped them on the haunches and drove them to the rear. All the time the farm burnt lower and lower, the jumping flames reflected in the moat adding a savage grandeur to the scene.'*

As the night wore on the Battalion took up defensive positions east of Bleu in support of 10 and 11 East Yorkshire Regiments. However, early in the morning of 12 April the enemy attacked in force and by sheer weight of numbers forced back the troops on each flank. The Battalion fought from ditch to ditch and hedge to hedge under furious enemy fire until ordered to fall back to the line of Ferme du Leet to Ferme du Bois. From there, despite point blank machine gun and artillery fire, the Battalion fought the enemy to a standstill. This gave relieving units valuable time to reform behind the Battalion.

At 11.30 am the Battalion retired in good order, in spite of the intense enemy fire, and a fresh line was taken up along the road running west from Haute Maison. The 10 East Yorkshire Regiment formed up on their left. The Battalion was then ordered to advance to Bleu and link up with units of 29th Division, but this proved impossible. By then the enemy was reported in Outtersteene and as the left flank of 10 East Yorkshire Regiment was exposed, a further retirement was made to the line of Ferme Labis to Ferme Lynde.

The night of 12/13 April was comparatively quiet and the opportunity was taken to strengthen the positions. At 8.30 am the enemy attacked in force but the Battalion held its ground. The enemy attacked again at 11.30, with again no success. A third attack came at 2.30 p.m. and again it was driven back. It was a desperate battle, with heavy casualties on both sides. At dusk orders came from 92 Brigade

From Ferme Lynde looking towards Bleu (Bleutour) from the crossroads D23/D69. *(The Pals Collection)*

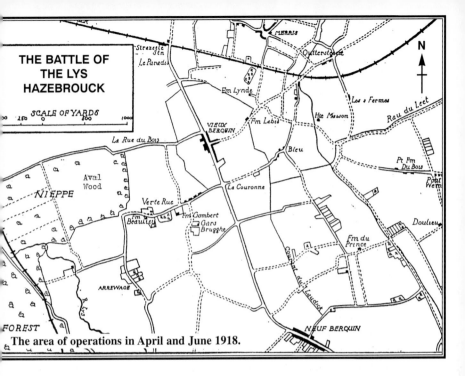

The area of operations in April and June 1918.

HQ to withdraw as the right flank was becoming exposed. The Battalion took up positions with the right flank on the Vieux Berquin to Le Paradis road about 700 yards (640 metres) north east of Vieux Berquin and the left flank on the railway line.

By midnight on 13/14 April Australian reinforcements arrived so at 4 am 92 Brigade withdrew to the support line. The Battalion, now totally exhausted, marched to billets at Pradelles then to Hondeghem, north west of Hazebrouck, for a much needed rest. Casualties had been so heavy that it was necessary to temporarily amalgamate the Battalion with 13 York and Lancaster Regiment of 93 Brigade to form 94 Composite Battalion. This new unit moved to Hazebrouck on 17 April and took over the town's defences.

L/Cpl. Crabtree's mind was on more basic matters.

'A group of us were billeted in an evacuated house on the outskirts of the town. When we explored the house we discovered, along with other vegetables, a sack of potatoes. Our lunch that day was – Bully beef, mashed potatoes and roast potatoes, carrots and leeks. As we were demolishing these good things, the lady of the house returned. "You perfidious English, you eat all my potatoes, my lovely carrots and leeks!' She was pacified however, when she saw the house had not been looted.

103

She actually had lunch with us before collecting articles of value to take away with her.'

The day after (19 April) the Battalion relieved 8 Australian Infantry Battalion in the now fast-stabilising line south west of Vieux Berquin. L/Cpl Crabtree:

> *'There was no direct road to this part of the line so we trudged along the railway side and came to Petit Sec Bois, where H.Q. settled down. The aid post was in an isolated farm across the fields. It was another untouched house teeming with good things to eat. The line was fairly quiet and we had time to scrounge and cook our plunder. Our stay was marked by good feeding. One effort was a huge potato pie, with a crust made from flour and bacon dripping. It was a great success and our American doctor sent his plate back for more – "Gad, you fellows, this is sure a swell dish. What do you call it?", said he.'*

L/Cpl. Crabtree's remarks about this doctor are worth quoting.

> *'Capt. F. W. Moeller, of the United States Medical Service, was a genial giant from Chicago, a first-rate surgeon and an expert on Obstetrics and Gynaecology. His gifts as a gynaecologist were utterly wasted of course, but he was a much beloved M.O. because he understood men and could treat them with sympathy and kindliness, virtues often lacking, even among comrades. He also knew more ways of playing Patience than any man in the British Army.'*

The Battalion was relieved on 28 April and returned to billets near the Australian C.C.S. at Hondeghem. The Battle of the Lys, as the German breakthrough became known, was over. As the Regimental History says, (page 552),

> *'By their prompt action on the morning of the 12th, and by the stubborn way in which they clung to their positions on the 13th in the face of three direct assaults, the 11th East Lancashire can surely claim to have taken no small part in helping the 31st Division successfully to accomplish its mission. During these two days of incessant fighting the Battalion had been compelled to fall back four times, each time in obedience to the orders of higher authority and not once by the dictation of the arms of the enemy.'*

Praise comes no higher.

The tremendous work done by the Battalion, and the courage and devotion to duty involved, is illustrated by the following extracts from award citations:

Major Lewis Hewitt Lewis – Distinguished Service Order:

'On many occasions whilst in command of the rearguard during two days hard fighting the conspicuous services of this officer were of the utmost value. His organisation of patrols undoubtedly saved a very difficult situation. Later on, under heavy machine gun fire, he was able to arrest a retirement that might have assumed serious proportions, but he rallied the men – and put them into good positions – and this resolved a very critical situation'.

Captain Francis G. Macalpine – Military Cross:

'By his fine example and personal courage he saved a very critical situation, collecting stragglers and consolidating a position under close fire from the enemy'.

Lieutenant Harold Wilton – Military Cross:

'When the whole of the troops in front had retired through the Battalion he prolonged the line to the left with his company. Although his flank was exposed and he was under point blank artillery and machine gun fire, he delayed the enemy by forcing them to consolidate. On three occasions he held on until ordered to retire. On three occasions he repelled enemy attacks'.

L/Cpl William Alexander Stuart – Military Medal:

'A signaller, he established communication by salvaging wire, and although the telephone wire was constantly broken, he never failed to repair it, thereby maintaining communications between Battalion H.Q. and company H.Q.s. His efforts undoubtedly contributed to the success of the defence.'

The Battalion lost three officers and thirty-three men killed. Nine officers and 149 men were wounded and forty-seven were missing. Forty-four men (which must include some men posted as missing) and 2/Lt. Reginald Blake are commemorated on the Ploegsteert Memorial, north of Armentieres. (It wasn't until 1991 that the name of 31522 Pte. Lawrence Ingham was added).

Eight men lie in Cinq Rues British Cemetery, Hazebrouck, a cemetery started during the battle and used until August. There are seven, including 2/Lt. John Cyprian Lott, MC, buried in Outtersteene

Ploegsteert Memorial, north of Armentieres. *(Mr Bob Curley)*

Communal Cemetery Extension, Bailleul. In Pont-du-Hem Cemetery, La Gorgue, there are 1,706 graves. Many of these are of men re-interred from twenty small burial grounds in the area after the Armistice. There is here a memorial to 26604 Pte. Charles Papworth, whose grave was destroyed during later operations.

Of the men who died of wounds, three are buried in Ebblinghem Military Cemetery, two lie in Boulogne Eastern Cemetery, and one each in Aire Communal Cemetery, Arneke British Cemetery and Longuenesse Souvenir Cemetery, St. Omer.

30572 L/Cpl. Harry Dorning died in a London hospital and his parents buried him in the family grave in Stockport Cemetery, Cheshire. There are sure to be others who, in the weeks and months ahead, died as a result of their wounds.

Following the Battlefield Trail

It is not possible to follow the 'trail' of the Pals during this period with any accuracy but some idea can be gleaned starting with the arrival of the Battalion at Le Paradis on 11 April 1918. The following, on a daily basis, indicates their subsequent movements in the area.

Day one of the battle – 11 April
Le Paradis: On D947 from Stazeele to Vieux-Berquin (just south of rail-way line). Follow D947 through Vieux-Berquin, turn left onto D69 to Bleu (Bleutour on modern maps).

12 April
Ferme du Leet and Ferme du Bois are not marked on the map (but see sketch map for Ferme du Bois). Haute Maison is on an unclassified road running due south of Outtersteene.

14 April
The march from Vieux-Berquin area to Pradelles. Take D947 to Stazeele and turn left onto N344 to Pradelles.

15 April
Continue from Pradelles on N344 to Hazebrouck and turn right onto D53 to Hondeghem.

19 April
The Battalion returned to the area to Petit Sec Bois. At Le Paradis (D947), turn onto the D53 (signposted Grand Sec Bois and Petit Sec Bois).

The most suitable maps to use are:
General map: Michelin No.236 Nord 1:200000
Local map: I.G.N. France 24.04 Hazebrouck ouest 1:25000.

4. Aval Wood – June, 1918

'The Battalion came out of the line near Caestre on 21 May, being heavily shelled on the way. Buses were waiting and as

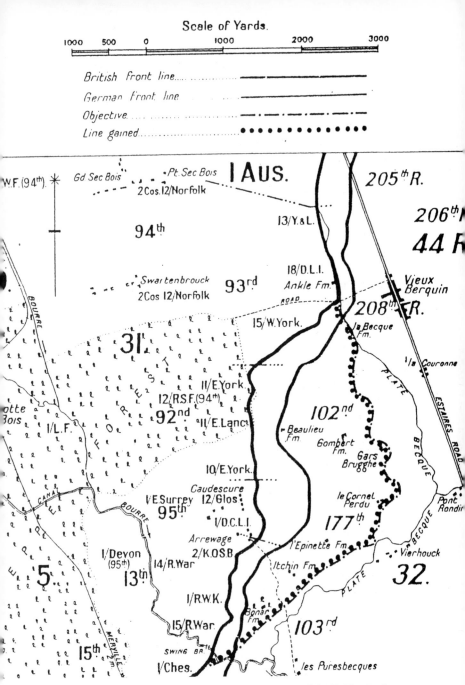

Scale of Yards.

British front line.............. ────────
German front line............. ────────
Objective.................... ── ── ── ──
Line gained.................. ●●●●●●●●●●

W.F.(94ᵗʰ) ✳   Gd Sec Bois ··· ·Pt. Sec Bois   **I AUS.**   **205ᵗʰ R.**
                    2 Cos. 12/Norfolk
                                    13/Y.&L.   **206ᵗʰ**
         94ᵗʰ   **44 R**

                  Swaitenbrouck   **93ʳᵈ**   18/D.L.I.   Vieux
                  2 Cos 12/Norfolk   Ankle Fm.   Berquin
                                    ROAD   **208ᵗʰ R.**
                          15/W.York.   la Becque
     31   Fm.
                                                              la Couronne

                          11/E.York.
                  12/R.S.F.(94ᵗʰ)   **102ⁿᵈ**
     92ⁿᵈ   11/E.Lanc.   · Beaulieu
                                      Fm.   Gombert
                                              Fm.   Gars
                          10/E.York.   Brugghe
                     Caudescure
     V.E.Surrey 12/Glos   le Cornel
     95ᵗʰ   Perdu   Pont
                  V/D.C.L.I.   **177ᵗʰ**   Rondir
                  Arrewage
     I/Devon 2/K.O.S.B.   l'Epinette Fm.   Vierhouck
     (95ᵗʰ) 14/R.War   Itchin Fm.   **32.**
     5 **13ᵗʰ**
                  I/R.W.K.
                          Bonar
     15ᵗʰ   15/R.War.   Fm.   **103ʳᵈ**
            SWING BR.
            I/Ches.   les Puresbecques

**28 June 1918. The front line before Hazebrouck, scene of the Pal's attack
on the German Salient at Beaulieu Farm.**

these were loaded up with men they moved off, in the semi-darkness, away to the west. The lines of buses rolled through Hazebrouck, Arques and St. Omer to Lumbres – the last few miles in the brilliant moonlight of a moon nearly at full. Tents awaited us at Divisional reserve in the Val de Lumbres and army life became almost the same as the happy training done in England before we went overseas. A fortnight here passed all too quickly.'

Thus L/Cpl Crabtree describes a long awaited rest, albeit including musketry and specialist training.

On 8 June the Battalion marched in blazing heat through Wizernes, Blendecques to Racquinghem. When they arrived, covered in dust, many men were feverish with temperatures up to 103 F. It was Spanish Flu, and for a few days it incapacitated the whole Battalion.

It was 15 June before the Battalion were fit to march to Wallon-Cappel into Corps reserve in readiness for a possible German attack on the Hazebrouck defences. This did not take place so on 21 June they relieved 2 South Wales Borderers of 29th Division in the line at Swarten-Brouck just north of the Bois de Aval (Aval Wood) in the eastern part of the Foret de Nieppe (Nieppe Forest).

On 25 June the Battalion came out of the line to the hamlet of Le Grand Hasard, on the Hazebrouck to Aire road. Here, preparations were being made for a local offensive by 5th and 31st Divisions on 28 June.

There were two main reasons for the proposed attack. The Germans had a salient just east of Aval Wood so it was necessary that attacks should be made, to the north and south simultaneously, to straighten the line. The second object was to push the British front line forward, clear of the immediate outskirts of the Nieppe Forest, the outline of which gave the enemy a very effective target for artillery registration. On 26 June a rehearsal was carried out at Pont du Papote, approximately half a mile (0.75 km.) from Le Grand Hasard. The Regimental History later commented:

'The closing stages were somewhat marred through the enemy putting down a heavy, destructive, shoot at the imaginary final objective. This gave a touch of reality to the proceedings which was neither helpful nor desired.'

At 6 a.m. on Friday 28 June the Battalion, with 10 East Yorkshire Regiment to the right and 11 East Yorkshire Regiment on the left, advanced behind a protective barrage towards its objective. The ground was quite flat, with corn waist high in places, but intersected

German machine gun team in action.

by hedges and ditches. Behind these, in shallow trenches and shell holes, were German machine gun posts. Speed and surprise were the keys to success, for if the enemy machine guns were allowed to come into play, there would be little hope of the attack succeeding.

Z Company, under the command of Captain Fleischer, attacked Beaulieu Farm, a veritable nest of such machine guns. In spite of fierce resistance the farm was soon captured. Capt. Fleischer, with great gallantry, personally rushed a machine gun post which was holding up the advance. One of his officers, 2/Lt. Fuller, also charged a machine gun post, killing the occupants. Then, with Sergeant White, his platoon sergeant, he rushed the next machine gun post. After Sgt. White was killed, 2/Lt. Fuller shot the enemy gunner with his revolver and captured the gun. In their courageous attack Z Company inflicted many casualties on the enemy and captured several machine guns and minenwerfers (trench mortars).

In the meantime, W Company, under Captain McKenzie, equally courageously captured Gombert Farm. Captain McKenzie, after all his officers were killed or wounded, reached Gombert Farm with only thirty-one men left. He then consolidated the position and held it for almost forty-eight hours in the face of an intense and almost continuous bombardment by the enemy.

In the attack on Gombert Farm Private Dixon carried ammunition for his Lewis gun team. When he saw the No.1 of the team killed he

Gombert Farm, the objective of W Company. *(The Pals Collection)*

immediately picked up the gun and continued forward. He was soon the sole survivor of the team. Despite his load of eight pans of ammunition and his rifle, he set up the Lewis gun, under heavy fire, and opened a flanking fire on a party of the enemy. He caused many casualties and so enabled a machine gun post to be captured.

As W and Z Companies held their objectives, X and Y Companies, under Captain Bentley, passed through them. Whilst doing so, Cpl. Ashton of X Company saw an enemy machine gun post in a hedge in front. He crept along another hedge at right angles, then threw bombs which put the gun out of action. He led his platoon on to capture the post. His platoon officer and sergeant were then wounded so Cpl. Ashton led the men to the final objective and consolidated under shell fire.

Y Company and the remainder of X Company meanwhile reached the Battalion's final objective. This was the line from the farm at Gaers Brugghe on the right to the hamlet of Verte Rue on the left (see map). Captain Bentley, though wounded in the head, refused to hand over his company until the position was consolidated. By now the Germans were withdrawing.

During this time Cpl. Bradshaw of H.Q. company was responsible for the signal lines from H.Q. to the forward companies. All through the attack he made repeated efforts, always under heavy machine gun and artillery fire, to maintain the connections. He worked continuously, and successfully, in these conditions for eight hours at a stretch.

Behind the lines, in Aval Wood, L/Cpl Crabtree worked at the Regimental Aid Post. His only later reference to 28 June was:

Beaulieu Farm looking towards Nieppe Wood on left. Objective of Z Company. *(The Pals Collection)*

Regimental stretcher bearers have a brief rest at the Aid Post.

'All day long wounded men, German and English, were carried to the shelter of the wood, whilst the walking wounded streamed past for hours. German prisoners were used to carry the stretcher cases further to the rear, and very happily they did it. Some of the prisoners handed over cigars to their captors, so we medical staff, besmeared with the blood of friend and foe alike, enjoyed a cigar in the brief periods of respite from bandaging the wounded'

An item in the *Nelson Leader* of 7 February 1919 told a rather different story when the Mayor of Nelson presented L/Cpl. Crabtree with the Military Medal.

'This is what your general says, he began, *"During an attack on 28 June 1918, L/Cpl. Crabtree persistently dressed the wounded under heavy shell and machine gun fire. For thirty-six hours he worked without food, shelter or sleep and it was due to his untiring and gallant efforts that our wounded were dressed and evacuated so quickly".* There is also a hint of other brave deeds. The Mayor continued, *'Also, in the rearguard actions of March (Ayette) and April (the River Lys) his work was beyond all praise and received the special notice of the Brigadier General.'*

After forty-eight hours of almost continuous heavy fighting the Battalion was finally relieved in the line by 24 Royal Welsh Fusiliers. They moved back to Le Grand Hasard into Divisional reserve. There, the Battalion received many messages of congratulations for its gallant conduct. Brigadier General O. de L. Williams, 92 Brigade Commander, told them he held them in such high esteem he had selected them to attack where he knew the most formidable opposition would be. It was a compliment they could have done without. W Company had been down to thirty-one men at one time and X Company had had thirty-four men left, under the command of a sergeant. The Battalion lost two officers and forty-four men killed. Seven officers and 194 men were wounded, of whom at least eight men later died. Eleven men were missing.

Both officers and forty-three men are buried in Aval Wood Military Cemetery. The cemetery lies on a bend of the D69 road near Verte Rue, just over a mile (approx. two kms.) west of the village of Vieux Berquin. Plot I was started by the Battalion and 11 East Yorkshire Regiment at the time of the battle. Plots II and III were added after the Armistice when over 300 bodies were brought in from the surrounding battlefields. Plot I, however, is second only to Queen's Cemetery, Puisieux, for the number of Battalion graves.

Le Grand Hasard Military Cemetery has three graves dating from that time. Two officers killed on 25 June 1918 when X Company H.Q. received a direct hit, and a sergeant killed on 28 June. Of those wounded in the offensive, seven died in hospital in St. Omer and are buried in Longuenesse Souvenir Cemetery nearby. 18058 Pte. John Wilson died in hospital in Wimereux, near Boulogne, and was buried in Terlincthun British Cemetery.

The total advance of the Battalion in the attack was a remarkable 2,000 yards (1,830 metres), the first forward movement made in 1918. A total of twelve machine guns, three minenwerfers and two pieces of artillery were captured.

The congratulations of the high command were complemented by the award of the Military Cross to **Captain Spencer Richard**

Aval Wood Cemetery. The site of the Aid Post. *(The Pals Collection)*

Fleischer and **2/Lt John Norman Fuller**. **Captain Cyril McKenzie** received the Military Cross to add to his Distinguished Service Order. **Captain G W H Bentley** was awarded a Bar to his Military Cross earned at Ayette in March. **37849 Pte Frank Bradley Dixon** and **26493 Cpl James Albert Ashton** were each awarded the Distinguished Conduct Medal for their part in the attack. The Military Medal went to **16201 Sergeant Wilfred White** (posthumously) and to **15400 Cpl Russell Bradshaw** and, of course, to **24799 L/Cpl Percy Crabtree**.

At the same time two men of Z Company were Mentioned in Despatches. The Adjutant, Captain F.C. Macalpine, wrote to all Company Commanders, 'Recommendations for Honours and Awards for half-yearly Despatch will be called for shortly by Brigade. Please forward to me particulars of any W.O.s, N.C.O.s or men whom you consider worthy of being recommended either on account of bravery under fire or good work behind the line. The nature of the services rendered will be indicated'.

In reply Captain Bart Endean forwarded the names of 26771 Pte. Donald Maclean and 26306 Pte. John Whelan. Of Maclean, he wrote,

DISTINGUISHED CONDUCT MEDAL

Awarded to – 26493, Cpl.A.Ashton, E.Yorks.Lancs.

Date– 28-6-18.

Action– For great gallantry and courage during an attack In action.

Commanding XI Co

(Mr R Ashton)

'This man as a Lewis Gunner has shown exceptionally good work during the past months. During the recent operations, this man, when his section commander became a casualty, took charge of the Lewis Gun section and used his gun with good effect against the enemy.' Of Whelan – *'This man has shown exceptionally good work as a Lewis Gunner. Twice during recent operations this man, after objectives had been obtained, went out under heavy shell fire to salvage Lewis gun magazines to replace those lost by casualties during the taking of the*

Cpl R Bradshaw (on left) awarded the Military Medal. *(The Pals Collection)*

*objective, in order to render the position held by his section more
secure against enemy counter attacks.'*

With a range of awards from the Military Cross to Mentions in
Despatches (of which, no doubt, there were many more), the 'local
offensive' of 28 June 1918 was not the last of the Battalion's actions,
but it was certainly one of the finest.

The Battalion spent much of July in Corps and Divisional reserve.
Even then, the war was never far away. L/Cpl. Crabtree observed:

*'We found a good bathing pool in the River Bourre and we
thoroughly enjoyed ourselves in it. It was rather awkward
though, when some sleepy German gunner, roused from his
afternoon nap to fire off a few rounds, dropped his shells into the
water amongst the bathers.'*

A village church painted by L/Cpl Crabtree whilst in Divisional reserve.
(The Liddle Collection)

Following the Battlefield Trail

Day one of the Battle – 26 June 1918

The Battalion came to Le Grand Hasard crossroads on the D916 Hazebrouck to Aire road. They had come out of the line at Swarten-Brouck, a hamlet on the unclassified road joining with the D188 from La Motte-au-Bois to Vieux-Berquin. (This road runs along the northern edge of the Nieppe Forest (Foret de Nieppe)).

26 June

Pont du Papote, the area of the rehearsal, is north of Le Grand Hasard, between the D916 and the junction with the unclassified road to Papote, a hamlet just north of the Nieppe Forest.

28 June

The area of the attack can be reached from Vieux-Berquin by following the D947 south. Turn right onto the D23. The D23 bears left at the junction with the D69 and passes Ferme Gombert on the left. Gaers Brugghe is just on an unclassified road to the left of Le Cornet Perdue. (The unclassified road continues to the D947).

On the D69 from it's junction with the D23, the first junction on the left going towards Verte Rue is the access road to Ferme Beaulieu. Continue through Verte Rue and, just before the road turns sharply to the left, is Aval Wood Cemetery. From the cemetery, with one's back to Nieppe Forest, one can look towards the battlefield.

The most suitable maps to use are:
General map. Michelin No.236 Nord 1:200000
Local map: I.G.N. France 24.04 Hazebrouck ouest 1:25000.

5. Ploegsteert – September, 1918

The Battalion War Diary records that the Battalion came out of the line north of Nieppe on 13 September 1918 and were moved by bus to the Divisional reserve area south of Hazebrouck. On 24 September, after rest and recuperation, no doubt with more training, they went by train from Hazebrouck to Bailleul and from there marched to billets near Neuve Eglise.

Meanwhile, other units of 2nd. Army were also moving forward in readiness to launch an attack on a front from Ypres to Armentieres on 28 September, one of a series of offensives which were to lead to the total withdrawal of German forces and the end of the war.

The Battalion assembled on Hill 63, on the north west corner of Ploegsteert Wood, during the night of 27 September, in readiness for the attack the following day. Battalion Operations Order 132 stated simply,

'It is thought the enemy may withdraw from the Messines Ridge and in the front of this sector. If this occurs, an attack will

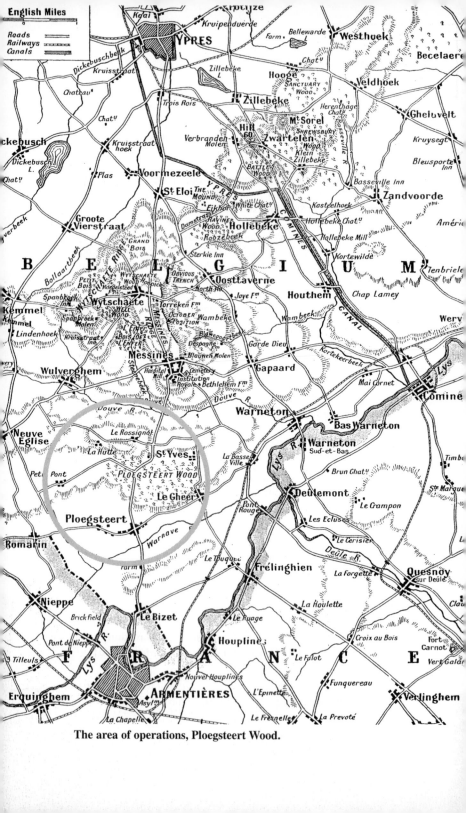

The area of operations, Ploegsteert Wood.

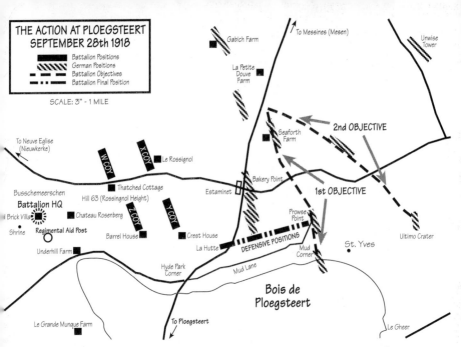

THE ACTION AT PLOEGSTEERT
SEPTEMBER 28th 1918

Battalion Positions
German Positions
Battalion Objectives
Battalion Final Position

SCALE: 3" - 1 MILE

Gabich Farm

To Messines (Mesen)

Unwise Tower

La Petite Douve Farm

To Neuve Eglise (Nieuwkerke)

Seaforth Farm

2nd OBJECTIVE

W.COY.

X.COY.

Le Rossignol

Bakery Point

1st OBJECTIVE

Busschemeerschen

Battalion HQ

Thatched Cottage

Hill 63 (Rossingnol Height)

Estaminet

Brick Villa

Chateau Rosenberg

Z.COY.

Y.COY.

Prowse Point

Shrine

Regimental Aid Post

Barrel House

Crest House

Underhill Farm

La Hutte

DEFENSIVE POSITIONS

Mud Corner

St. Yves

Ultimo Crater

Hyde Park Corner

Mud Lane

Bois de Ploegsteert

Le Grande Munque Farm

To Ploegsteert

Le Gheer

Plan of the Battalion attack. (Based on Captain Endean's original trench map) *(Mr Tony Bell)*

> be ordered. The Battalion will attack with 10 East Yorkshire
> Regiment on the right and the 2/16 London Regiment (30th
> Division) on the left". In the Order each company was allocated
> an assembly position, a formation for attack and an objective.
> (see map).'

The Second Army's attack, to the north of Ploegsteert, began at 6 am.
It was calculated that the force of the main attack would compel the
Germans to evacuate the Messines and Ploegsteert Wood areas. In
anticipation of this, and to pressure the Germans to do so, the
Battalion, with the other units of 92 Brigade, was to await the order to
attack. At about 11 a.m., the battalion got the order, 'Z Hour is 3 pm'.

German shells bursting in Ploegsteert Wood. *(Taylor Library)*

Bart Endean (on right seated) with fellow officers of Z Company.
(Mr Tony Bell)

The plan was for X and Y Companies to capture the line from Prowse Point to Seaforth Farm, after which W and Z Companies were to leapfrog through to the second objective beyond the village of St. Yves (St. Yvon). (see map). The attack was to take place under a protective, creeping, barrage of artillery.

Captain Bart Endean was in command of Z Company. Together with W Company they followed X and Y Companies in the advance.

'At zero hour we advanced. Very little shelling. We walked down the hill, across the Messines to Ploegsteert road and through a hedge. I was carrying my revolver in my right hand. Just as I walked across the field, I could see a German at the end of a trench, about three hundred yards (275 metres) away. I watched him pick up his rifle and put it on the parapet of the trench. I'd no idea he was going to take a pot at me. But he did! It didn't stop me, it just sort of turned me sideways. I dropped my revolver and my right hand disappeared up my sleeve. I said, "Bloody hell! what's the matter here?". I pulled the hand down with my left hand and up it went up my sleeve again. I sat down in a shell hole. Somebody took my tunic off and put a bandage on, but as I stood up the bandage dropped off. 'I walked back to

BATTALION HEADQUARTERS

SITE OF REGIMENTAL AID POST

The site, just beyond Underhill Farm Cemetery, of the Regimental Aid Post. Battalion Headquarters was in the house on the skyline. *(Mr John Kingsmill)*

Battalion H.Q. (see map), to the Medical Officer at the Regimental Aid Post, and my wound was dressed. I was put on a stretcher, on a trolley, and was wheeled away down the road to where ambulances were waiting. I was eventually dumped down inside the entrance to a marquee at 64 Casualty Clearing Station. There were people a lot more seriously wounded than I was so it was midnight before I was operated on.'

Capt. Endean may not have realised it, but it was the end of the war for him.

Meanwhile, as Captain Endean was at the Aid Post, the capture of the second objective could not be attempted as the attack by 10 East Yorkshire Regiment on the right, had failed. Also, on the left, the attack by the 2/16 London Regiment was only partially successful. Because of this the Battalion was forced to form a defensive flank on the road from Prowse Point to La Hutte, north of Hyde Park Corner. By then it was holding a salient almost 3,000 yards (2,750 metres) in depth on a base of 2,500 yards (2,300 metres) The salient was strongly, and persistently, attacked with machine gun and artillery fire from the north east and the south, but the Battalion held its ground, in spite of heavy casualties.

Fortunately, the main attack further north continued to succeed throughout the day and on 29 September the Germans were forced, as anticipated, to retire from Messines and the line at Ploegsteert Wood. The Battalion was then relieved by the 10 East Yorkshire Regiment and 18 Durham Light Infantry and withdrew to Brigade reserve near Hill 63.

In spite of everything, the Battalion took fifty prisoners. They also captured a field gun, an anti-tank gun and seventeen machine guns. The Battalion paid dearly in casualties. A total of 353 officers and men

A row of Pals in Underhill Farm Cemetery. *(Mr Bob Curley)*

were killed, wounded or missing in one day's fighting. Thankfully, 28 September was to be the last day on which lives would be lost on such a scale.

Underhill Farm Cemetery is near the site of the Regimental Aid Post. It is by the roadside, opposite the farm from which it takes it's name, about half a mile (800 metres) west of the Ploegsteert Memorial. Sixteen men of the Battalion are buried here. One is Pte. Fred Leeming 15774, of Great Harwood, the last of the 'original Pals' to be killed in action. His grave number is D44. Next to him in D43 is 2/Lt. John Holden, one of two officers killed that day (2/Lt. Thomas Henry Clarke lies in grave D24). 2/Lt. Holden was a native of Oswaldtwistle. At the outbreak of war he was twenty-five and a moulder of cast iron at Howard and Bulloughs, an Accrington engineering works. He enlisted in the 2/5 East Lancashire Regiment (Territorials), quickly becoming a sergeant and in October 1917 was gazetted a 2/Lt. He transferred to the Battalion in the Spring of 1918.

After 2/Lt. Holden's death Lieutenant Colonel Rickman wrote to his parents. It was a fine tribute to the Battalion as well as to their son.

'...*I almost at once recognised his capabilities and appointed him second in command of his company. I regret to say he was killed instantly by a machine gun bullet whilst gallantly leading his men in the attack In the short time he was with us he endeared himself to all and his fine leadership was a splendid example to all. The Battalion has received fine mention for its part in the battle and all the credit was due to the splendid gallantry of the men who, like your son, have given everything for their country. We all regret so much the loss of your son. I*

*almost at once noticed his power of command and his fine
leadership With deepest regrets, Yours sincerely, A. Rickman
Lieutenant Colonel'*

Four men also killed on 28 September are buried in Strand Military
Cemetery, Poegsteert Wood, on the Ploegsteert to Ypres road. A further
six are commemorated on the Tyne Cot Memorial, Passchendaele.

After Captain Endean was treated at 64 Casualty Clearing Station
he was moved to 5 Red Cross Hospital, Wimereux, north of Boulogne.

*'I stayed a couple of nights and then I was put on a train for
a hospital ship to England. On the ship they asked us where we
were from and where we would like to go to. I told them there
was a military hospital near my home in Newcastle. I finished up
in Epsom, Surrey. I was in hospital there when the Armistice was
signed. From Epsom I went to a hospital in Moffat, in Scotland,
until finally I was transferred to Newcastle. I ended up in
Armstrong College, then temporarily a military hospital, in the
same room where I had gone for drawing and clay-modelling
classes before the war.'*

The injury to Capt. Endean's right shoulder, above the arm-pit, resulted in a 30% disability pension for life. It was often painful and the
damage to the tendons restricted the use of his right hand. In spite of
this, he became a skilled stonemason and remained a talented artist
until his death in 1990.

L/Cpl Crabtree must have returned to the Battalion after 29
September because he was with Z Company when the Battalion was
relieved by 15 West Yorkshire Regiment at Warneton on the River Lys
on 4 October 1918.[1]

*'As we left the line we tramped over the shoulder of Messines
Ridge, which the Battalion had helped to capture a few days
before. The gigantic mine crater was still there, the ground all
churned up into a maze of shell-holes. Naked desolation seemed
to haunt the place.*

*'We entered Ploegsteert Wood again and marvelled at the
blasted trees that had put forth leaves again. Nature seemed to
be continuously covering up man's diabolical handiwork as the
seasons advanced. Flowers had grown again, long grasses in the
Summer had half hidden some trenches, while the flashing red of
thousands of poppies had spread across the old battlefields in a
blaze of colour making fitting memorials to the thousands lying
beneath.*

'It was with such thoughts we marched back through the

wood. The new moon was not visible, making progress oftimes difficult, while some sank to the knees in mud when they stepped off the road. A halt was made at a derelict farm where we learned that Neuve Eglise was our next billeting place. Here, we knew, was a hastily constructed camp with gaping holes in the huts that allowed draughts to whirl about like small hurricanes.

'After dinner on 6 October we marched through Neuve Eglise (Newchurch in English – reminding some of us of the little village close to Pendle Hill, near Burnley) to a camp on the outskirts of Bailleul and into Brigade reserve.

'It was on the north side of the town, near the ugly brick Lunatic Asylum. "We've getten to't reight shop at last", said some wag.'

1. Percy Crabtree seems to have missed the action at Ploegsteert. He refers only to 'returning' to the Battalion at the end of September. He was almost certainly wounded – something he rarely mentioned in later life.

6. Ambush at Wattrelos – October, 1918

At 8 o'clock in the morning of 18 October 1918, the Battalion arrived in Turcoing, an industrial town of 80,00 inhabitants, as the Germans were retreating out of the eastern suburbs. They got a rapturous welcome. Church bells which had been silent under four years of occupation rang out to greet the troops.

An hour later the Battalion entered Wattrelos. Again there was no opposition. However, as Y Company marched along the Rue Leruste, a local woman ran to tell them of a group of German soldiers hidden behind a hedge further ahead. Surprisingly, her warning was ignored, and they continued on their way.

Moments later there was a solitary burst of machine gun fire. Four of the leading men were killed outright. Two officers and sixteen men

The Rue Leruste, taken from the German side, probably from where the machine gun was posted, note the church on the left. *(M Georges Rachaine)*

Rue Leruste from the British side. Note the church on the right. It is believed a German lookout was in the church tower. *(M Georges Rachaine)*

were wounded. The concealed machine gunner had waited for the shortest possible range. In spite of the ambush Y Company continued to push the German rearguard out of Wattrelos.

The next day the Battalion buried its dead. The ceremony took place in the Cretinier Cemetery, 1,000 metres from Rue Leruste. The four graves were covered with flowers by Wattrelosiens, who attended in large numbers. (Flowers are regularly placed on the graves to this day).

The dead were: Sergeant Philip Foster of Accrington; Cpl James Gelling of Nelson; Pte Walter Grimshaw of Clayton le Moors and Pte Horace Masser of Newport, Monmouth. Their graves are numbered 11, 10, 8 and 9 respectively. (Pte. Michael H. Nicolls of Leicester died of his wounds on 19 October and is buried in Mouvaix New Communal Cemetery. 2/Lt. Mark T Washbrook of Manchester, died in a Boulogne hospital on 21 October. He lies in Terlincthun British Cemetery, Wimille, in Grave No X1 C 32).

Six days previously Cpl. Gelling had written the following letter. Understandably, he was in good spirits. Dated 12 October 1918:

> *'Dear Mother, Just a line to let you know I'm still on Fuller's Earth and well and hoping this finds you the same. You will see from the heading that I have been further promoted to full Corporal. I want one more and I shall be Sergeant. I am once more in 'B', you will know where I mean – where I came home from last time. Expect me at the end of this month or the beginning of next. I have some good news to tell you. I have been recommended for a medal for good work in the trenches. I don't know what it*

123

Cpl J Gelling.
(The Pals Collection)

will be, either a Military Medal or a Distinguished Conduct Medal, but I would not say anything until you hear about it. I was slightly wounded in the head but I did not go into hospital. It was alright the next day. Well, I will close now. With love to all at home, from your loving son, Jim. xxxxx.'

The next letter Mrs. Gelling would receive would be the following: Dated 31 October 1918, it was from Captain A. H. B. Stansfield, O.C. Y Company.

'Dear Mrs. Gelling,

It is with deepest regret that I have to inform you of the death of your son 18411 Cpl. Gelling J.

He was killed in the recent operations of 18 October 1918 having been shot by a bullet fired by an enemy sniper.

He was a good soldier and a very promising N.C.O. and his loss is keenly felt by the Company, who all mourn the loss of one of their comrades.

We are forwarding to you the Divisional honour and certificate which he won in conjunction with the Military Medal, and we are sorry we were unable to present it to him before his death.

Yours truly, A. H. B. Stansfield, Captain.'

7. Last Men Killed in Action – November, 1918

During the first week of November 1918 the Battalion continued to follow the German forces as they withdrew deeper into Belgium.

On 8 November the Battalion took over, from the 12 Norfolk Regiment, a line of posts on the west bank of the River Schelde (Escaut) near Avelgem. Y Company were encamped in a farmyard on the outskirts of the village.

On 10 November L/Cpl J. S. Royden wrote to the wife of 49267 Pte. Peter James Johnston:

'Dear Mrs. Johnston, I am writing these few lines to express the sympathy of the platoon and myself with you on the loss of your husband, Pte. Johnston. It will be a small relief to you to know that he did not suffer any pain, as he was killed instantly, with one of his comrades, whilst on sentry duty on the night of the 8th inst.

It need hardly be said that Pte. Johnston was most popular amongst us, and performed all his duties, even the most arduous, cheerfully and without complaint.

You may rest assured that he will receive a fitting burial and

This photograph shows a part of Roubaix as the Pals would see it in October 1918. *(M Georges Rachaine)*

> *that he will not be forgotten. In repeating, on behalf of your late husband's comrades, our profound regrets in your bereavement, believe me to be, Yours very sincerely, J. S. Royden.'* [31461]

A friend of Pte Johnston, Pte Ray Donald in an undated letter described to Mrs. Johnston what happened,

> *'...we had been moving for two or three days and on this*

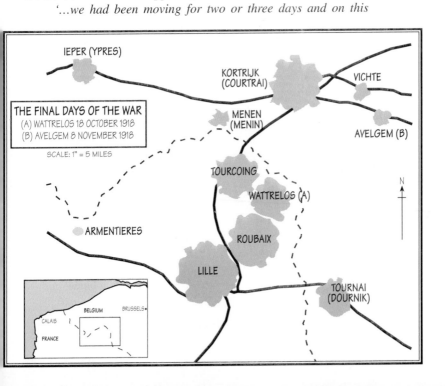

night (8 November) we stopped at a farm. Your husband and a lad named Kneen were the first on sentry duty. Jerry was shelling at the time and a shell dropped right beside the gate and killed them both instantly. I had to go on sentry at the same place and it was the longest night I've ever spent. We were to move forward in the morning but we all went to see them before we left. They were both laid on stretchers – we had to leave them.'

Pte. Peter James Johnston of Carlisle and 39624 Pte. William E. Kneen of Liverpool were buried where they fell. A rough wooden cross marked their grave.

On 22 May 1919 the Infantry Records Office at Fulwood Barracks, Preston, sent Pte. Johnston's personal effects to his widow. They included photographs, letters, a wallet and coins,etc. (The wallet and photographs had been pierced by a shell splinter).

On 10 June 1919 the Infantry Records Office informed Mrs. Johnston that her husband was buried 'north east of Avelgem, nine miles east south east of Courtrai'.

On 1 December 1920 the Infantry Records Office sent a short note to the effect that,

'It has been found necessary to exhume bodies in certain areas', and 'the body of Pte James Johnston has been removed to the cemetery stated below – Vichty Military Cemetery, 3/4 miles west of Vichte and 5 miles east north east of Courtrai.'[Note error in forename]

Pte Johnston (circled) in training at Crosby near Liverpool in 1917. He originally enlisted in the Border Regiment. *(Mr Johnston)*

Vichty Military Cemetery. *(Mr John Kingsmill)*

On 9 March 1925 the Imperial War Graves Commission wrote to Mrs. Johnston asking for the cemetery register details to be confirmed and also for any required personal details to be included in the register entry. Mrs Johnston did not reply.

Pte. Peter James Johnston's grave number in Vichte Military Cemetery is III D 5. Pte. William E. Kneen's is III D 6.

8. Armistice Day – Percy Crabtree

'On Sunday, 10 November, the Medical Officer told us that an armistice would be signed on the morrow. No one believed him. Somehow, though, the day seemed different. Jerry was either short of ammunition or he had cleared out, for only occasional shells came over. We marched eastward through Renaix to a small village called Bosstraat and there billeted for the night.

'At dawn we were ready to advance, but no orders came until nearly nine o'clock. News came through that fighting would cease at eleven o'clock and the Battalion's movements, or lack of them, seemed to substantiate the rumours.

'Just before eleven o'clock the Battalion halted. Here was something we never dreamt would happen – a cessation of hostilities. The surge of thoughts was so utterly bewildering that many men trembled as they spoke, relief and fear alternating rapidly in their minds.

'The fateful hour came, and there descended on that vast battlefield a stunning silence. Thoughts were too deep and sacred for utterance. It seemed as if God's peace had suddenly swept over the land, and there rose on the breeze that dispersed the November mist countless prayers of thankfulness echoed by millions of people in every land where men had marched away.

'Then the silence was broken, emotions were stifled in typical British fashion and some wag shouted "It's all over boys, bar the shouting". "But", answered his pessimistic pal, "Who's won?"

'Soon after eleven o'clock, the Battalion marched on,

following the retiring Germans at a distance, frequently halting for unknown stoppages somewhere ahead. Three miles further on, at Everbecq, a small cortege of French dragoons were carrying a hastily constructed coffin, containing the body of a comrade killed a few minutes before eleven that morning. As they filed into the village church, the inhabitants and all the soldiers stood to attention, while from the church the organ played a funeral march that struck a respondent note in the heart of many a man standing by.

'Before dusk the Battalion reached Grammont on the River Dendre, a tributary of the Scheldt. Here English prisoners of war rested for the night on their return march from captivity. The Germans too, were held up here, by the terms of the Armistice, and the Battalion withdrew to Geoferdinge, a village about a mile to the rear.

'Z Company was billeted in a convent, and that night supper was cooked by the nuns. The Mother Superior, a middle-aged lady with a finely modelled face, knew Lancashire, having lived there for some time, and she wished for us to sing some of the English songs she had heard and loved years ago.

'This put us all on our mettle. For an hour we sang lustily, yet tunefully, many of the English favourites, as well as hymns and carols. In many of the latter the nuns joined in, adding soprano and contralto to the preponderance of base and tenor. Here were Roman Catholics, Anglicans, Baptists, Methodists and other nonconformists singing with light hearts to celebrate the coming of peace.'

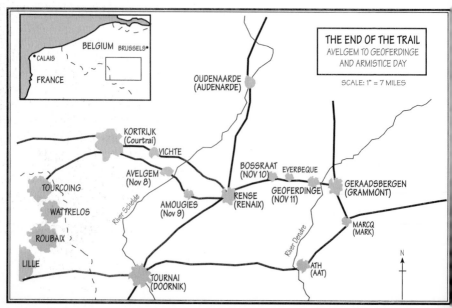

CHAPTER FIVE

The Pals Industry

Introduction

In July 1996 a *Guardian* journalist wrote an article headed, 'Friends of the dear old Pals' in which he coined the phrase 'Pals Industry'. This described the work done – and which continues to be done – by the Tourist Information Centre, the Local Studies Library and St. John's Church in Accrington to further the memory of the Pals.

In addition, Benjamin Hargreaves Primary School in Accrington has its own 'Pals Project' as part of its curriculum (also now done by other schools in the area). Finally, Mr. Peter Whelan, the noted playwright, inspired by Martin Middlebrook's T*he First Day on the Somme*, wrote the extremely popular play, *The Accrington Pals*.

The following contributions are each a personal view of their part in the 'Pals Industry':

1. **Helene Heyes - *The Tourist Information Centre***
2. **Helen Barrett - *The Local Studies Library***
3. **Revd. Dennis Crook - *The Pals Chapel, St. John's.***
4. **Enid Briggs - *A School's Pals Project***
5. **Peter Whelan - *The play*, The Accrington Pals**

1. Helene Heyes - *The Tourist Information Centre*

Accrington has had a networked Tourist Information Centre since 1990, although Hyndburn Borough Council have provided an Information Centre dealing with local tourism since the mid 1980s. In April 1997 the Lancashire County Council Information Centre, merged with the Tourist Information Centre and this then became the Accrington Information Centre.

Helene Heyes
(The Author)

Visitors and residents usually know three things associated with this area: Accrington Stanley Football Club; Accrington 'Nori' Brick and the Accrington Pals.

An ever increasing number of the queries we deal with are from people who are interested in the Pals and want to obtain further information.

With this in mind, it was decided that the Council should produce its own Accrington Pals Leaflet in association with Accrington Library. The leaflet contains a brief history of the Pals, information regarding The Pals Memorial Chapel at St.

John the Evangelist Church, an 'Accrington Pals Town Trail' and details of museums, events and books associated with the Pals. The leaflet was launched on 1 July, 1992, at the Pals Chapel with the Mayor, Cllr Mrs Cathleen Thom together with Mr William Marshall, who at 99 was the last surviving Pal. The leaflet has been an outstanding success and has been reprinted on an annual basis.

In 1993, Bill Turner lent the Tourist Information Centre a slide of a patriotic postcard that the Pals sent to their family and friends when they were training at Caernarfon, Wales, during 1915. We asked local photographer, Alfred Hoole to take a photo of the Pals Chapel and the two shots were used to produce the Pals Postcards. Again, these have proved to be very successful.

Accrington Town Hall underwent extensive renovation work during 1993, prior to the relocation of the Tourist Information Centre in November of that year. The new Centre is now on the site of the original Council Chamber where the Pals Battalion was raised in 1914. We thought that we should draw the public's attention to this, and so a plaque was placed in a prominent position which states:

To Commemorate
The 11th (Service) Battalion (Accrington)
East Lancashire Regiment (The Accrington Pals)
Was formally raised in this room
(The former Council Chamber)
By the Mayor of Accrington, Councillor John Harwood
On the 7th day of September, 1914
Unveiled by William Turner, November 11th 1994

Peter Whelan's play The Accrington Pals is performed regularly throughout the country and we often receive requests from theatre groups, both professional and amateur, who wish to visit the area and see for themselves the places that the Pals knew and to visit the Pals Chapel, the War Memorial in Oak Hill Park and of course the Local Studies Department of Accrington Library. The Pals leaflets have been used by many of these groups to enable their audiences to learn more about Pals.

Our next project regarding the Pals came about from a member of the public who called into the Information Centre and noticed that we sold commemorative plates relating to the mining industry which was once so prevalent in this area. He asked whether he could get one about the Accrington Pals?

The *Accrington Pals Commemorative Plate* was designed by ourselves and was launched on 1 July, 1995. It features the Pals Memorial in Serre, Regimental Colours & Drum. The local towns and villages where the Pals came from are featured on the side of the plate. The reverse has a brief history of the Pals. The plate is a limited edition of 650 and we have received requests from throughout the UK and also from France & USA.

1996 was the 80th anniversary of The Battle of The Somme and our largest and most successful project to date was the "The Accrington Pals Exhibition", which was held in the Town Hall. Originally the exhibition was scheduled to run during the month of July. However the response from the public was such that we had to extend the run of the exhibition throughout August as well. Over 1000 people a week came to view the exhibition and as the Visitors Book showed, they came from throughout the country. Many overseas visitors who were in this area staying with family and friends also came to the exhibition.

The exhibition was organised in conjunction with Accrington Library. The pupils from Benjamin Hargreaves Junior School brought in their Accrington Pals Project for the exhibition. Each pupil 'adopted' a Pal and wrote about them, this included poems, prayers and pictures. Their contribution was very moving and was a highlight of the exhibition. We asked the public for any material they might be willing to loan us for the exhibition and we were amazed by the response. Items were brought in on a daily basis throughout the two months that the exhibition was open. Blackburn Museum kindly loaned us a German Maxim Machine Gun which was captured in 1918 by the Pals, the Regimental Museum also loaned various artefacts. Quite a few items brought in by the public were donated to us and these are now held in our Cellar Exhibition area which is opened to the public as part of our regular guided tours of Accrington Town Hall.

The Information Centre staff are also asked on a regular basis for details regarding accommodation and places to visit in the Somme, especially Serre. Following on from the success of the exhibition, it was decided to send a member of staff to the Somme to learn at first hand more about this region. The trip was led by Bill Turner and apart from visiting the cemeteries and memorials connected with the Pals, we left information relating to the Pals and Accrington at all the major Museums, Hotels and Tourist

Information Centres as part of our service to tourists and battlefield historians alike.

The Accrington Pals Exhibition underlined to us the importance of keeping the memory of the Pals alive. To this end the Information Centre stocks not only our own items but various other items which are connected to the Pals and the Battle of The Somme, e.g.

Accrington Pals Book (W. Turner) (Pen & Sword Books Ltd.)

Accrington Pals Remembered (A guide to their last resting places & memorials) (W Turner)

The Somme Battlefront Pack (P.R.O.)

Army Service Records (P.R.O.)

Battleground Europe – Serre Book (J. Horsfall) (Pen & Sword Books Ltd.)

Lapel Badge (East Lancs Reg.)

Keyring (East Lancs Reg.)

Accrington Information Centre
Town Hall
Blackburn Road
ACCRINGTON
Lancashire
BB5 1LA

Tel: 01254 386807 I 872595 Fax: 01254 380291 e-mail: - leisure@hyndburnbc.gov.uk
Internet: - http:/www.newsquest.co.uk/llt/hyndburn/

2. Helen Barrett B.A. A.L.A. – World War One Collection of Accrington Library

Helen Barrett
(The Author)

Accrington Library may seem to some to be a surprising place for a major collection of some 1500 volumes of literature on World War One. The collection dates back to the 1950's when subject specialisation schemes were adopted in public libraries. This ensured, as far as possible, the complete coverage by an individual library, of a particular subject. Local industry, culture and local history were the criteria for deciding each library's allocation and so Accrington came to specialise in World War One.

In 1974 Accrington library became the District Library for the new Hyndburn authority and the decision was made to continue the W.W.1 specialisation, but with a slightly different emphasis and with selective purchase. As the publication of books about the war continues the purchase of everything is not possible. Accordingly, a policy evolved of acquiring material which would enable researchers to trace individuals, whilst at the same time major histories would not be ignored.

The Collection is housed in three separate departments. General books about the war, narratives, poetry, biographies etc. are shelved in the Lending Library and the storeroom: the Reference Library has the C.W.G.C. registers, official histories and research material and the Local Studies Library concentrates on material relating to the 'Accrington Pals', and to a lesser degree other Lancashire regiments.

The 'William Turner Pals Collection' is held on deposit in the Local Studies Library. This is a unique collection of photographs, newspaper cuttings, tape recordings, memorabilia and documentation, complete with a card index. The collection has been used extensively by researchers, television producers, journalists and family historians.

A feature of the Local Studies Library is a 9ft. by 6ft. photograph of 3 and 4 Platoons of 'A' Company of the Pals. This was used by the Octagon Theatre, Bolton, in their production of the play 'The Accrington Pals' in 1982. Since then the library resources have been used many times by professional and amateur companies staging the play. Library staff maintain a file of posters, newspaper cuttings, theatre programmes and recordings of the play.

The Local Studies Library has a microfilm file of the Accrington Observer and Times from 1887 to date. Rolls of Honour of local men appear regularly from February 1915 and in 1919 the newspaper published a booklet The Greater Accrington Roll of Honour. When used in conjunction with The Accrington Pals Remembered by William Turner there is an almost complete list of the local war dead.

A recent addition to stock is an A4 file in three volumes, giving personal details of the 851 Pals (one page per man) who died during the war. A complete list in C.W.G.C. cemetery alphabetical order of all men of the East Lancashire Regiment (including the Pals) buried or commemorated at home or abroad is also available to researchers.

Military books in stock relate specifically to Lancashire unit and regimental histories. There is also a complete set of volumes of the Pals series by Pen and Sword Books. Pupils of a local

Primary School have produced Poems about the Accrington Pals. *Based on their Pals project, the poems are especially poignant and a credit to the children and their teachers. In 1996 the Public Record Office released to the public a quantity of W.W.1 army service records. To mark the occasion a pack of facsimile documents entitled* Battlefront *was published. The pack includes personal documents relating to a Private James Barnes of the Pals. Also shelved are video tapes relating to the Pals, including a 1915 newsreel.*

Also available are the Absent Voter *lists of the* Electoral Registers. *From February 1918 servicemen registered in order to have a vote. The information provided by the serviceman consisted of name, number, regiment corps or ship and service address. This is often of great value to the family historian.*

Also of value is Soldiers died in the Great War 1914-1918 *on microfilm. Over 667,000 names are listed and each entry includes name, number, place of enlistment, place of residence and the date of death. The precise place of death is not given – only the country. It's companion publication is* Officers died in the Great War, *also on microfilm. A 1988 edition in book form contains twelve pages of names previously omitted.*

The Reference Library has a complete set of the C.W.G.C. registers of cemeteries and memorials throughout the world. These ensure that a grave or name on a memorial can be traced and some biographical information obtained.

The C.W.G.C. registers were used for the Cross of Sacrifice *series, published by S.D. and D.B. Jarvis. The series provides a list of officers who died in the service of the British Commonwealth and colonial countries. There are over 60,000 names with supporting details. Royal Marine deaths are recorded in* With Full and Grateful Hearts *published in 1991. 6,261 deaths are noted, covering the period August 1914 to October 1919. There are also three 'Rolls of Honour' (Hood, Howe and Nelson Battalions) of the Royal Naval Division, published by the Imperial War Museum. These give personal details and number, date of death and theatre of war where death took place. War casualties of the Royal Flying Corps and the Royal Air Force are in* Airmen died in the Great War *by Chris Hobson.* Soldiers Killed on the First Day of the Somme *by F W Bell is another useful reference. Other volumes relate the histories of various regiments and divisions.*

It can be said that the pride of the Collection is The Official
History of the Great War, *in 75 volumes. This is a scholarly work,
the purpose being 'to provide within reasonable compass an
authoritative account, suitable for general readers and for
students at military schools, of the operations of the British Army
in 1914 - 1918'.*

*The Collection also contains many volumes of personal
memoirs and accounts of warfare on land, at sea and in the air.
A large number of these are rare and unusual volumes dating
from the 1920's and 1930's.*

*The Reference Library also keeps current information on
travel to, and accommodation in, the battlefields area and the
staff will be happy to deal with enquiries.*

*The Library staff believe that the W.W.1 Collection will enable
them to offer a service to researchers equal to, if not better than,
most public libraries in the North West.*

*For anyone wishing to use the World War One Collection the
address is:- Accrington Reference Library, St. James' Street,
Accrington, BB5 1NQ, Lancashire. Tel. 01254 872385, Fax.
01254 301066.*

3. Revd. Dennis Crook A.K.C. - The Pals Chapel, St. John's Church

*Who would have thought that a pipe organ in need of
restoration would have led ultimately to the creation of the Pals
Chapel in the church of St. John the Evangelist, Accrington?*

*The story begins with the discussions surrounding the organ
– should it be repaired or perhaps a different scheme
considered? Eventually it was agreed that a magnificent organ
of 1906 (by T. C Lewis) for sale in Glasgow should be purchased.
However it was suggested to us that the organ should be placed
on a platform in the north transept. The old organ was sold and
removed, but two wooden panels were retained to preserve a link
with the past. Indeed, many generations of choristers had left
their initials upon them. Two such unknown boys had, however,
written – 'Pals in church 21st February 1915' and 'Toke (sic) in
action at Sir (sic) July 1st 1916. Heavy casualtys' (sic). These
words were to serve as the inspiration for the 'Pals Chapel.*

*The Lewis organ was duly re-built and the area underneath
was cleared of its pitch pine pews. Demanding and urgent
building work placed great claims upon parish resources, but the
publication of Bill Turner's book turned my thoughts to the*

problem. Bill had discovered that the Pals had used the church for their final service before they left the town – so what could be more appropriate than the siting of a permanent memorial to the Battalion?

It had long been my dream that the church should have a side-chapel; a place of quiet, a still place for smaller Eucharistic services, and the daily saying of morning and evening prayer. I based my ideas on the chapel at Whalley Abbey which had been designed with a central altar with seating on three sides for the congregation. As I read Bill's book I realised that there was no one place where the Pals were commemorated. So here was the long awaited opportunity to develop the north transept for the benefit of parishioners and the wider community.

Mr. Christopher Martindale, a distinguished ecclesiastical architect was commissioned to design the chapel. The plans were fully discussed over twelve months and it was agreed that the chapel was to be primarily a place where services and prayer were to be offered on a daily basis. It was not to be a memorial chapel in isolation from the rest of the church but an integral part of it.

The style and design reflect these fundamental principles. The paving of Portuguese stone (English Hoptonwood stone proved to be too expensive) provides a quiet foundation for the richly moulded mahogany stalls. Between the panels and above the pews are seven plaques and banners representing the infantry regiments of Lancashire at the time of the Great War. The eighth (the York and Lancaster Regiment) had a close connection with the Accrington Pals.

The dignified memorial tablet was carved by John Shaw of Accrington and the small cross by Jack Haworth of Hollins School. Other items of interest include the Toc H lamp donated by the Accrington branch. However, particular mention must be

The Pals Chapel. *(Hyndburn B.C.)*

made of the drum. It was used as the troops marched between villages in France and was left behind the lines as battle raged. Miraculously, the drum was preserved, along with the drumsticks and was presented to Lt. Col. Rickman in 1919. After his death it remained in the possession of his son, Major Gerry Rickman. He most movingly and generously presented the drum to St. John's at the dedication of the chapel on 23rd. February 1992.

Since 1992 the chapel has received further beautification and mention must be made of Mr. Alfred Hoole and R. P. Townley, the main contractors. The late Mr. Clifford Collinson was also in the forefront of raising the £30,000 needed for the chapel. Donations have come from public bodies and private individuals – many of whom had a personal link with the Pals.

A great surge of interest came as a result of the church and chapel appearing on the 'Songs of Praise' BBC TV programme for Remembrance Sunday 1991. Hundreds of letters were received and visits by groups and individuals arranged, many of whom were pleased to see the names of relatives recorded in the special Book of Remembrance. A steady flow of visitors from home and overseas have been welcomed at the church.

There is an annual service on the Sunday nearest to the 21st of February when the British Legion standard bearers from many branches lead the standards of regimental and other organisations in dignified procession through the church. The silence surrounding the Act of Remembrance which focuses particularly on the Pals is a moving and poignant reminder of our past history. We owe a debt to them which we can never repay.

Yet, as I knelt many times before the altar with faithful congregations I was frequently aware that we did not worship alone. In the chapel, facing the same altar, gather those whose names are recorded in the Book of Remembrance. They cannot be seen, but somehow you know they are there, their eyes are God-ward like yours and that your act of worship is an act fully shared with them.

There can be no greater justification for the planning and building of the chapel. I hope that those who come to kneel before the altar and those who make an act of family pilgrimage will be able to sense that we are sharing our communion with a mighty host, for we indeed meet with 'angels and archangels and with all the company of Heaven'.

4. Enid Briggs - A School's Pals Project

My husband's uncle, Walter Briggs, was an Accrington Pal, and died on 1st July, 1916. His family was badly affected, and my father-in-law would never talk about him: only the publication of Mr. Turner's books encouraged my husband and I to find out more.

We now feel so strongly that the memory of the Accrington Pals should be preserved that we have put together a project for Top Juniors at Benjamin Hargreaves' C.E. Primary School, Accrington. To give them a feel for the times, the children learn first about pre-war Accrington, and Walter's family and home life. We then move on to the outbreak of war, concentrating on how Walter and members of his family felt: the pride and patriotism of his father, the fears of his grandfather, the emotions of his fiancée and older sister, as her fiancée, too, goes off to fight, the confusion of his younger brother – the crowds cheer as the soldiers march away, yet his mother weeps in anguish.

At this point, every pupil takes on the identity of a real Accrington Pal. The choice of Pals has to be carefully worked out, to ensure the correct proportion – how many died, how many were injured, how many have no known grave, how many returned home to die, how many survived but died in later engagements, etc.. I choose Pals whose pictures can be found in one of Mr. Turner's books (with the exception of three Pals

Pupils of Benjamin Hargreaves Primary School, Accrington, look at part of the display designed and made by them as part of their Pals project. Their teacher, Susan Brown and Fred Cook, Rector of Accrington look on.

Photograph by kind permission of the Editor, Lancashire Evening Telegraph.

connected with St. Paul's Church, whose pictures can be found in newspapers). Except that I might allow particular friends to be 'brothers' the identities are given out at random: as in 1916, these Pals have no control over their fate.

The children learn briefly of the progress of the war, concentrating on the reasons and preparations for the Somme offensive. They learn about life and conditions in the trenches, but all written and art work is undertaken from the point of view of 'their' Pal. They write letters, prayers and diaries, constantly examining how these men and their families at home must have felt.

1st July itself takes a full morning, and the mood is sombre. Much use is made of eyewitness accounts and attempts are made to indicate the scale of the casualties.

The next day, the children assemble in the school hall. By this time, many will have discovered 'their' fate, but each formally gives his name and is consigned to a group. The atmosphere is tangible as the groups of 'killed in action' 'killed in action, no known grave', 'wounded', grow.

I stress to them that these are the true proportions. Before the exercise, I ask the Class Teacher to choose at random six 'Pals' whom she, as an ordinary Accrington woman, might have known – a son, a neighbour, the butcher's boy, etc.: at the end of the exercise, the outcome is often that she would not have seen any of them again. My husband is a keen photographer, and, as we have visited the Somme region many times, I am able to give each 'Pal' who dies a picture of his gravestone or of Thiepval.

We then consider the reactions at home – the delay in receiving news – my own mother's story of women hearing news from injured soldiers leaning out of a train, and running round to her parents' shop in distress. We look at newspaper coverage, telegrams and letters, parents' appeals for news, the horrors and uncertainty behind the word 'missing'. Throughout, I use precious articles from our own family, and I tell the effect of Walter's death on each – how his grandfather died soon after, his mother never laughed again, his brother could never speak of him without tears.

We then move to the theme of Remembrance, and the work of the CWGC and the British Legion. The children are encouraged to visit Pals' graves at Accrington Cemetery, noting the Cross of Sacrifice, and the War Memorial in Oak Hill Park. Earlier in the *project, they visit the Chapel at St. John's Church (seeing, on the way, incidentally, the place where the news-bearing train was standing)*

The culmination of the project is a Remembrance Service in St. Paul's Church on either 1st July or 11th November, incorporating eyewitness accounts, the children's work and traditional items, and conducted entirely by the children. Poppies are worn by all, and the Church is suitably arrayed. We have been privileged to welcome civic leaders, representatives of the British Legion and local historians, as well as parents and members of the church community: many are in tears.

I believe the children when they say of the Accrington Pals,
'WE WILL REMEMBER THEM'.

N.B. The most recent project resulted in the publication of a booklet, "Poems about the Accrington Pals". This is available from the Headteacher, Benjamin Hargreaves Primary School, Barnfield Street, Accrington, price £2.50.

5. Peter Whelan - The play, The Accrington Pals

It's over fifteen years now since I first had the idea of writing 'The Accrington Pals' for the theatre......and I still recall vividly how it came about.

I'd never visited Accrington until I wrote about it......though when I did I was struck by the kinship with the Potteries where I grew up. Both are close, compact, industrial communities set amongst high moorlands, visible above the rooftops and at the end of streets. Both had (do they still?) an active Primitive Methodist movement I was part of it myself long ago.

Peter Whelan
(Copyright Julia Painter)

My parents came from Salford and for some years before 1980 I'd wanted to write a play about them when they were young in the First World War. My father was in the Manchester Regiment and my mother, for a time, became a forester, sent on active service to chop down trees in Sussex!

The nub of the idea came when I read Martin Middlebrook's 'The First Day on the Somme', a pulverising account of Britain's awakening to machine age violence.

One short paragraph caught my imagination. It concerned what happened in Accrington after the battle...how townspeople, driven desperate by rumours of disaster and angered by ludicrously optimistic reports in the press, marched to the mayor's house to demand the truth.

Some have since told me that this never happened, though Martin always stoutly maintained that it did. For me it set the

140

mood for a play about those left behind when the Pals went off to war. It was to be a play about the tensions of resisting authority and the tragedies of upholding it...and a play about the most basic divisions between us all, putting politics on a personal level.

Above all, it was to be a fractured love story between a strong minded, individualistic woman and a dreamy young socialist who joins the Pals. It was also to be a play about a community of women, recognising that the doors that opened for them in that war gave tantalising glimpses of freedom, as well as scenes of horror.

Writing the play put me in touch with a few of the surviving Pals and two of them were able to come to the opening of the production in London. Since then it has been widely performed in New York, as well as in major British theatres. An adaptation was broadcast on Radio Four and there have been constant amateur productions over the years.

It is the play that very much encouraged me to persevere as a playwright. So, you can imagine, I have a lot of affection for it.

N.B.
Performing rights
Amateur rights are handled by Samuel French Ltd., 26 Southampton Street, Strand, London WC2E 7JE.
The script of "The Accrington Pals", by Peter Whelan is published by Samuel French Ltd, is obtainable from the larger bookshops, price £5.50 (1997) ISBN 0 57311 00 93.

Biographical Note

Peter Whelan was born in the Potteries in 1931. After National Service and Keele University he made a career in advertising together with short film scripting before writing full-time for the stage. His first solo play was 'Captain Swing', a story of the revolt against agricultural machinery. Then, in 1981 came 'The Accrington Pals'.

Peter Whelan's other works, most of which were for the Royal Shakespeare Company, include 'The School of Night', a play about Christopher Marlowe; 'The Herbal Bed', about Shakespeare's daughter Susanna; 'Divine Right', about republicanism in a future England and 'Overture', a play about the ugliness of the modern world.

TOWN TRAIL

1. St. Johns Church
2. The Coppice
3. Oak Hill Park
4. Acc. Town Hall
5. Acc. Info. Ctr.
6. Acc. Library
7. Berkley
8. Globe Centre
9. Sacred Heart
10. Ellison's Tenement
11. St. James Church
12. 5 Whalley Road
13. Whalley House

HYNDBURN RD
EASTGATE
HOSPITAL
ADDISON ST
BURNLEY ROAD
KING STREET
BLACKBURN ROAD
WHALLEY ROAD
MELBOURNE STREET
AVENUE PARADE
THE COP
BROADWAY
BLACKBURN ROAD
EAGLE STREET
SCATCLIFFE STREET
WILLOW ST
CANNON ST
ST. JAMES ST
PEEL ST
MANCHESTER ROAD
NOT TO SCALE
OAK HILL PARK

(Hyndburn B.C.)

The Mayor, John Harwood, takes the salute as the Battalion march past the Town Hall on 2 August 1915. *(The Pals Collection)*

CHAPTER SIX

THE PAL'S TRAIL IN ACCRINGTON

Introduction

There are, in essence, two Pals Trails. The first, the more detailed, is in the town of Accrington itself (see map page 142). The second, more of a list than a trail, covers the area around Accrington within the county of Lancashire.

Accrington itself has, of course, many places associated with the Pals whilst the rest of Lancashire has more artefacts, militaria and publications held in museums and libraries.

For no other reason that 'A' is first in the alphabet, the 'Pal's Trail' starts in Accrington:

1. St. John the Evangelist church, Addison Street, off Burnley Road, BB5 6AR.

The church has an unusual banded spire which is an important part of the town's skyline. It was built in 1866-1870 at a cost of £6,250. The seating capacity was originally 880 but is now 730.

The church has a wealth of stained glass windows, with the west window a particularly fine example of Victorian design and craftsmanship. The Ambulatory window is a stunning modern work by Tom Denney and the etched window in the porch door is an early work of Brian Clarke.

The Pal's Memorial Chapel is in the North Transept and seats a further thirty-five. The church was the scene, on 21 February 1915, of the last church parade held in the town before the Pals went to Caernarfon. On the third Sunday in February every year there is a 'Memorial Service' to the Pals.

St. John the Evangelist church.
(Local Studies Library Accrington)

St. John's own parish war memorial is a bronze tablet on the North wall. It bears thirty-five names. An oaken plaque nearby records eight WW2 deaths.

143

2. The Coppice

The Coppice, the hill which overlooks the whole of Accrington, can be reached from the top of Avenue Parade. An alternative way is from Peel Park Avenue, off Burnley Road. The flat top of the hill was the scene, in 1914 and 1915, of Company manoeuvres. Evidence of trench digging still remains.

Behind Peel Park Primary School, on Alice Street, just off Burnley Road, is a playing field now used for schoolboy football. This was the home ground of Accrington Stanley from 1919 to 1966.

(Local Studies Library Accrington)

3. The War Memorial, Oak Hill Park, off Manchester Road

In design, scale and situation the war memorial is one of the most impressive in the country. It is on high ground near to the rear entrance of the park from Hollins Lane. There are extensive views towards the Coppice and the eastern side of the town.

The memorial is a stone obelisk decorated with a figure representing Maternity mourning her children. It was unveiled on 1 July 1922. The honour of placing the first wreath - to the Pals - went to John Harwood. Eleven slate tablets set in the wall of the stepped base bear the names of 865 1914-1918 War dead. The adjoining 1939 - 1945 War memorial has 173 names.

4&5. The Town Hall and Tourist Centre, Blackburn Road BB5 1LA Tel. 01254 386807

This fine building was originally the Peel Institute, built as a memorial to Prime Minister Sir Robert Peel, a man of local origins. It became the Town Hall in 1865.

The Tourist Information Centre is on the ground floor, in the area that was, in 1914, the Council Chamber in which the Pals were raised by the Mayor, John Harwood. There is a plaque on the wall to this effect. Alongside is a framed photograph of Will Marshall, the last of the original Pals. A small shop sells books, postcards and other items relevant to the Pals. A display case in the foyer contains examples of

(Hyndburn B.C.)

militaria. There are photographs, maps (including trench maps), newspaper cuttings, etc. in a small exhibition room. Guided tours of the Town Hall take place every Thursday.

6. Accrington Central Library, St. James' Street, BB5 1NQ. Tel 01254 872385

The Library was built in 1907 with money provided by Andrew Carnegie (1835 - 1919) the noted philanthropist. In the library there is a wide range of books for lending, a recorded sound collection and many other public information services. The Local Studies Collection is on the first floor. Access to the Pals Collection is available on request. There is a comprehensive collection of books on the 1914 - 1918 War in the adjoining Reference Library. *(Local Studies Library Accrington)*

7. Berkley Restaurant and Banqueting Suite, Willow Street BB5 1LP

The building was a day school from 1864 and later became the Sunday School for nearby Cannon Street Baptist Church. During the 1914 - 1918 War several of the classrooms were used as a medical centre. The Pals who enlisted in Accrington were examined here. It continued as a Sunday School until 1970. In 1980 it was converted into its present use.

8. Globe Centre, St. James' Square BB5 0RE Tel. 01254 600608

In 1914 Globe Works, the textile engineering factory of Howard and Bulloughs, dominated the working life, and the skyline, of the town.

The company was founded in 1853 and became the town's largest employer, exporting textile machinery worldwide.

In September 1914 a large number of employees enlisted in the Pals. Some of these, however, were to return in 1915 as munitions workers.

(Hyndburn B.C.)

Over the years the industry fell into decline and after several changes of ownership, much of the works was demolished in 1995. The present five story Globe Centre is the only part remaining. The Centre houses a business resource centre, several Hyndburn Council offices, a brasserie, a restaurant and a ten bedroom hotel.

9. Sacred Heart Church, Blackburn Road BB5 0AH

The church was completed and consecrated in 1869, replacing the smaller church of St. Oswald's, built in 1852.

The High Altar is of outstanding quality. Designed by Pugin, it is

Gothic in form and richly carved in marble and Caen stone. The parish war memorial is a fine life-sized marble sculpture depicting the removal of Christ from the Cross. Formerly beneath the choir loft in the church, the memorial is now in the entrance porch. In this church, in 1914 and 1915, were held the church parades for the 148 Roman Catholic members of the Pals.

10. Ellison's Tenement, off Blackburn Road / Ellison Street.

A small area of land known to generations of Accrington people as the venue for travelling fairs, pot fairs and circuses. The Pals used the area as a daily parade ground, always watched by an interested crowd. In wet weather the newly constructed tram-shed nearby was used as a drill hall. This building is now occupied by a building firm. The Tenement is partly covered by extensions to the original tram-shed and bus-depot. The remainder is a car park and storage area for the building firm.

11. St. James' Church, St. James' Street / Cannon Street BB5 1NQ

The parish church of St. James was founded in 1546 as a chapel of ease for St. James' Church, Altham. It was rebuilt in 1763 and became the parish church in 1870.

In November 1938 the Pal's Colours were taken from the Town Hall, where they had been since 1919, to St. James' where they were formally blessed and laid up. In later years the white fabric of the Colours deteriorated so they were mounted in a glass case on the South wall in 1968.

12. Shop, 5 Whalley Road BB5

When recruiting for the Pals started in September 1914, the 'Orderly Room', or office, was in the Town Hall. A fortnight later an empty shop, formerly a pork butchers, was converted into a 'headquarters' and remained so until February 1915.

The shop has been the 'Barbara Kay' shoe shop since 1977.

13. Whalley House, 281 Whalley Road BB5 5AD

The home of the Mayor, John Harwood, until his death in 1923. It was here, on 6 September 1914, that John Harwood held the initial meeting with local businessmen which led to the raising of the Pals a week later. After 1 July 1916 many wives and mothers came to the house seeking information about the Pals.

The house is now a private residence for the retired.

CHAPTER SEVEN

The Pals Trail in Lancashire
Introduction

In 1914 the towns of east Lancashire were grimy milltowns with poor living conditions and much poverty. All have ancient beginnings, however, and a proud heritage. In the 1990s all are working hard to encourage new manufacturing and service industries and to improve the way of life for their townspeople.

The 'Trail' is in Blackburn, Burnley and Chorley with diversions to Preston and Clitheroe. There is also a visit to Manchester, a city in Lancashire in 1914 , but currently the administrative centre of the county of Greater Manchester.

It would not be practicable to have a 'route' as such. In any case each town has so many other attractions that the visitor will certainly be tempted to stay a little longer.

Each section which follows begins with a brief outline of the town's history and it's social and economic background as it was in 1914 or thereabouts and as it is in the 1990s. Then follows a description of places associated with the Pals.

BLACKBURN

Blackburn, five miles from Accrington, was the largest town in the area with an association with the Pals. Its contribution to the Battalion was the smallest: the 'Blackburn Detachment' of fifty men, part of 'C', later 'Y' (Chorley) Company. This was understandable in a sense because Blackburn was then the H.Q. of the 4th Battalion, East Lancashire Regiment, Territorial Force, as well as that of the 1st East Lancashire Brigade, Royal Field Artillery, Territorial Force (known as the 'Blackburn Artillery').

Blackburn is also the oldest town. Ancient records note a church here in the year 596 and there are traces of a Roman road. The Domesday Book tells us – "In Saxon times King Edward (the Confessor) held Blacheburne". (William the Norman, by right of conquest, of course, claimed the town). Although in an area of mostly uncultivated moorland, forest and chase, Blackburn was a thriving market town in the early sixteenth century. Indeed, according to a ballad of the day, "lusty lads from Blackburn" fought at Flodden in 1513. In the Civil War the town was Parliamentarian and the garrison defeated a Royalist attack in 1643.

In common with other Lancashire towns, Blackburn became a centre for handloom weaving, first of woollen and then of cotton cloth. During the nineteenth century the town was pre-eminent as a centre for the development of cotton weaving technology. It rapidly became a major producer of cotton cloth. By 1911, according to the last census before 1914, there was a population of 133,052. The town's other main industry was textile engineering (power loom manufacture). Blackburn was also a 'brewery town' with three large breweries.

The decline in the cotton industry started just before 1914. After the war Blackburn's dependence on weaving meant unemployment and poverty in later decades. In 1974 Blackburn joined together with Darwen and a number of surrounding villages to become the Borough of Blackburn with Darwen. In recent years Blackburn has encouraged a wide range of new industries to the town. Where once there was only weaving and its

The scene in 1998. Note the new Market Hall clock. *(The Author)*

King William Street, Blackburn on a market day circa 1914. *(Local Studies Library Blackburn)*

associated engineering there are now electronic components, acrylic and plastics, paint and wallpapers, footwear and office furniture manufacturers as the main industries. The Royal Ordnance Factory's Electronic and Precision Systems Division is also in the town. Blackburn's three nationally known breweries continue the brewing tradition.

Tourism is now an important industry. Two thirds of Blackburn is countryside – mostly open moorland but with some farmland and wooded valleys. Several country houses dating from medieval times attract many visitors. 'Witton Country Park', of 480 acres, is less than two miles from Blackburn centre. Next to the park is a major outdoor leisure area with an athletics track, show-field, equestrian arena and orienteering course. Leisure activities on this scale were unheard of in the days of the 'Blackburn Detachment'.

There is still a strong military connection with the town. Blackburn Cathedral, the only Anglican cathedral in Lancashire, is the venue for the annual commemorative service of the East Lancashire Regimental Association, held on the Sunday nearest 1 July. Known as 'Somme Day', the service commemorates all the men of the East Lancashire Regiment who lost their lives in two world wars.

Blackburn Cathedral, off Darwen Street. Tel. Cathedral office, 01254 51491.

There has been a church on the site since before the ninth century. A new parish church, consecrated in 1826, replaced one of fourteenth century origin. A hundred years later the newly created Diocese of Blackburn required the enlargement of the church into a cathedral. Work started in 1938 and the Cathedral was finally consecrated in 1977.

St. Martin's Chapel is the memorial chapel of the East Lancashire Regiment. Four regimental colours are suspended above the entrance and on the glass screen wall are etched the three soldier saints - St. George, St. Michael and St. Martin of Tours. Many of the chapel furnishings have been given in memory of individual soldiers. A brass plaque states that the stone altar is in memory of Pte. William Aspinall, an original Pal, killed in France on 29/3/1918 whilst serving with the Machine Gun Corps.

Blackburn Central Library, Town Hall Street BB2 1AG Tel 01254 661221

The Reference Library holds many WW1 titles. These include the

E.L.R. Association Journal 1955 and 1965 (two bound volumes) and The D.C.M. 1914-1920 Citations (East Lancashire Regiment).

'The Blackburn Times' and 'The Lancashire Evening Telegraph' are available on microfilm and hard copy. There is a card index of newspaper cuttings (with photographs) of men named in the Book of Remembrance held in the Old Town Hall. Several Pals are listed.

BURNLEY

Burnley was the home of 'D', later 'Z' Company, of the Pals. The town is five miles from Accrington in the mix of countryside and industrial town that is now described by the tourist industry as Lancashire's Hill Country'.

Burnley grew out of a village founded about 1122. There is evidence, however, of Bronze Age dwellers in the area. A market charter granted in 1293 gave added status to a developing town in the centre of a handloom

The scene in 1998. *(The Author)*

A quiet day in St. James' Street, Burnley circa 1914.
(Local Studies Library Burnley)

woollen weaving area. In the eighteenth century wool was displaced by cotton. By late Victorian times the town was at the heart of the Lancashire cotton industry and produced more cotton cloth than any other town in the world. Its other main industries of engineering and coal-mining were both associated with the cotton industry.

Burnley was not all industry however. In nearby rural Hurstwood 'Tattersall's House' was built by the family which went on to found the bloodstock auctions of the same name at Newmarket. Also in Hurstwood, in the mid-sixteenth century, lived Edmund Spenser the Elizabethan poet. Not far away, in Holme-in-Cliviger, is the burial place of General Sir James Yorke Scarlett, the leader of the successful charge of the Heavy Brigade at Balaclava on 25 October 1854.

Present-day Burnley is a much better place to live than in the years leading up to the war of 1914 to 1918. In 1911, for example, the infant mortality rate was 202/1000 live births. In 1996 the rate was 3.3/1000 (half the England and Wales average). In 1907 3,442 Burnley children aged ten to fifteen years were employed in the cotton mills - twenty years after child labour in the textile industry was banned in Austria, Germany and France. By 1914 the cotton industry was starting the decline which led to its eventual demise in the 1960's. Even as war broke out mills were closing. The war even worsened matters for Burnley because its looms were unsuitable for weaving khaki uniform cloth. A shortage of raw cotton brought further mill closures. The sound economic footing which cotton provided simply faded away.

Although the population of the town has declined from 106,331 in 1911 to 89,790 in 1996, Burnley is still a busy manufacturing town. Forty per cent of the working population are in industry. In place of cotton there is now bus and truck tyre manufacturing, automobile electronic systems design and manufacture, plastic technology and manufacture, a T.V. tube and glassware factory and several engineering works. There are also service based industries such as healthcare, insurance and mail order. The association with cotton remains. Burnley is the home of one of Europe's largest maker and supplier of home furnishings.

The smoky mill chimneys, cobbled streets, clogs and shawls image of the old days has gone. However, a part of the town once the hub of the cotton industry is now preserved as a tourist attraction. The area is one of the best preserved Victorian industrial landscapes in the country. The 'Weaver's Triangle' incorporates a working mill, warehouses and worker's cottages on a canal-side site. Tourism is now a major industry in its own right.

Burnley's associations with the Pals are as follows.

Burnley Central Library, Grimshaw Street, BB11 2BD Tel 01282 37115.

The Reference Library has a selection of reference books on WW1 subjects, with nothing specific about the Pals.

The local newspapers which cover the period - The Burnley News and the Burnley Express – are available on microfilm only. Just two relevant photographs are in the Photographic Collection.

A bound copy of the 'Greater Burnley Roll of Honour 1914 -1919' (4,100 names) gives the names and personal details of several members of the Burnley Company of the Pals.

Towneley Hall Art Gallery & Museum, Towneley Park, Burnley BB11 3RQ Tel. 01282 424213.

The Hall, set in 24 acres of wood and parkland, is thought to date from the 14th. century. The former home of the Towneley family, it was bequeathed to the town of Burnley in 1900. The rooms are furnished in period.

The East Lancashire Regiment Room has a small display of uniforms and swords dating from the 18th. century. There is a display of different types of medals dating from 1799 to 1914 - 1918. There are two portraits in oils of Burnley V.C.s of WW1. No material relating to the Pals is on display.

Burnley Boys' Club, Barden Playing Fields, Barden Lane, BB10 1JQ Tel 01282 424038

Burnley Lads' Club was established in 1899 by Mr. H. D. Riley to provide recreational and educational facilities for working boys. Many members of the club served, and died, in the 1914 - 1918 war - a number of them, including Mr. (Captain) Riley in the Burnley Company of the Pals.

In 1968 the Lads' Club amalgamated with the Burnley Police Youth Club to become the Burnley Boys' Club. In 1990 the club moved to it's present premises.

In the entrance to the club is a framed photograph of Capt. Riley and a framed scroll naming 123 members who died in WW1. A bronze tablet also commemorates the members who died in WW1.

The names of members who died in WW2 are on an adjacent wooden plaque. The most recent commemoration is of a member who died on active service in Bosnia in 1995.

CHORLEY

The market town of Chorley, sixteen miles from Accrington, seems an unlikely home for a company of the Accrington Pals. A local solicitor's own recruiting drive in August 1914 ended when the Mayor of Accrington (who had family and business connections with Chorley) accepted his two hundred men. These became 'C', later 'Y' (Chorley) Company.

Chorley, set between the moors of east Lancashire and the fertile Lancashire plain, has been a market town since at least 1498. In medieval times the town (Cherleigh in 1251), became an important trading centre for the agricultural producers of the area. In about 1750, in common with most Lancashire towns, hand-loom weaving of cotton cloth was introduced. By 1911, when the population was 30,315, cotton spinning mills, bleaching and printing works and their attendant coal mines dominated the town. In the 1990's, whilst agriculture still plays an important role in the area, those industries have all but disappeared.

2/Lt Rigby with 'Ned' the mascot, leads Chorley Company up Chapel Street on 23 February 1915. *(Local Studies Library Chorley)*

Today's major manufacturing employers are telecommunication systems (e.g. payphones) and electronics. The Royal Ordnance Factory produced millions of shells for the 1939 - 1945 war and

The scene in 1998. *(The Author)*

after and still produces much of Britain's supplies today although it's future is far from certain. A textile factory now manufactures sports and outdoor leisure wear. Even with these firms Chorley is less industry based than Accrington, Blackburn and Burnley. Manufacturing employs less than 20% of the population.

Chorley's location, served by a good network of road and rail, makes it ideal as a business and distribution centre for many national companies - hence 71% employed in the service and leisure industries. An illustration of the difference between the Chorley of 1914 and the 1990's must be 'Camelot', a mock medieval theme and adventure park, complete with live jousting tournaments, which entertains thousands of tourists every week.

The men of Chorley Company would know, however, the area's real heritage. Miles Standish, reputedly of Duxbury Hall, Chorley, sailed on the 'Mayflower' in 1620 (Duxbury, Massachusetts, was founded in 1630). Henry Tate of Chorley founded the sugar refining company, became a patron of British art and gave the nation the Tate Gallery. At nearby Hoghton Tower, in 1617, King James the First 'knighted' a loin of beef 'Sirloin'. Some say William Shakespeare worked as a tutor at Hoghton Tower as a young man.

In 1974 Chorley joined together with several villages in the surrounding agricultural area to form a new borough. In the 1990's the population of the new Chorley is three times that of the old. Much has changed since 1914, yet most streets in the town centre, although crowded and pedestrianised, would be recognisable to the 'Chorley' Company, and the 'Flat Iron' market, dating from 1298, would, of course, have the same busy character.

Pals material can be seen at:

Chorley Central Library, Union Street PR7 1EB Tel 01257 277222
The Local Studies Library holds local newspapers of the WW1 period on microfilm. These are: The Chorley Guardian and The Chorley Weekly News.

In the Photographic Collection are several photographs of individuals and groups of Pals.

Also held is a pamphlet, published in 1916, about the torpedo attack on the 'Ionic'.

Astley Hall, Astley Park, PR7 1NP Tel. 01257 262166.
The Hall is owned by Chorley Borough Council. It is just off the A6 road to Preston. The Hall has its origins in Tudor times and has been

much altered and added to over the centuries. In 1922 the then owner, Richard Tatton, donated the hall and ten acres of parkland to the people of Chorley as a War Memorial. This memorial is probably unique in being a house, a park and also having a Memorial Arch and a Memorial Cross within the grounds.

Inside the Hall is the Room of Remembrance. A roll of honour on oak panels records the names of the men of Chorley who died in WW1 . Items specific to the Chorley Company of the Pals are:-

1. A framed, illuminated, list of 55 men who died, and 158 who returned from the war.

2. A large framed photograph of the Company parading in the Devonshire Road Drill Hall on 23 February 1915.

3. A large framed photograph of the Company marching along Chapel Street on 23 February 1915.

4. A large framed photograph of the Company on parade in Union Street on 19 December 1914.

There are also three 'Golden Books' of the names and photographs of the men of Chorley who died in the war. One volume is in a display unit, its leaves turned daily. The men named on the illuminated list (see 1) are also featured in the 'Golden Books'.

PRESTON

Although not the county town, Preston is the administrative capital of Lancashire. County Hall, opened in 1882, holds the offices of the County Council. The Lancashire County Record Office is nearby.

The right to hold a 'Guild Merchant' was granted to Preston by Henry the Second in 1179. The occasion was celebrated irregularly up to 1542. Since then, with the exception of 1942, the 'Preston Guild' has been celebrated every twenty years. It is a week of festivities which brings together Prestonians from all over the world.

The Pals were unusual in that, in 1914, they were the only service battalion of the East Lancashire Regiment not to be formed at the Regiment's depot at Fulwood Barracks.

Lancashire County Record Office, Bow Lane, Preston PR1 2RE. Tel. 01772 263039. Fax. 01772 263050

The collection of documents is one of the largest of its kind in the country. The area covered is generally the post-1974 county of Lancashire.

There are three main types of record: Official - census returns, Quarter Sessions, etc.; Ecclesiastical - parish records, etc. and Family

- family, business and society records.

The parish records and census returns are useful for the family historian researching military ancestors. There are also books about Lancashire regiments and units in the library. There are no manuscript records and no items specific to the Pals.

The Museum of Lancashire, Stanley Street, Preston PR1 4YP Tel. 01772 264075. Fax. 01772 264079

The museum (formerly The County and Regimental Museum) is in the Old Sessions House. Built in 1825, the building was used as a court, a Territorial Army Royal Artillery H.Q. and a motor vehicle licensing centre before becoming a museum in 1986.

A large military collection includes a replica of a WW1 dugout, with a 'voice over' of L/Cpl. Will Marshall of the Pals describing his experiences on 1 July 1916. A display of documents relating to war service includes one concerning a Pte. Pickup of the Pals. Medals on display include two Military Medals, two Distinguished Conduct Medals and a Croix de Guerre awarded to Pals.

The museum shop sells a wide range of military history books. A 'WW1 Facsimile Document Pack' produced by the Lancashire County Museum Service, contains documents relevant to the Pals.

The Queen's Lancashire Regiment Museum, Fulwood Barracks, Preston PR2 4AA. Tel. 01772 260362

Fulwood Barracks is one of Preston's finest nineteenth century buildings. It has been an important military establishment since 1848. The museum holds a comprehensive collection of uniforms, weapons, medals and memorabilia covering the history of the Regiment and its forebears from 1689 to the present day.

The East Lancashire Regiment section of the museum has, in the library, several items relevant to the Pals. These include a trench map of 1916, photographs of groups and individuals, a photocopy of Sgt. P. Allsup's diary (Dec 1915 to July 1917) and an album of newspaper cuttings.

Also in the library is a complete set of the *Official History of the War (Military Operations)*, a complete set of the Army List and a complete set of the Regimental War Diaries.

The Regimental Shop sells many items – cuff-links, lapel badges, key rings, regimental ties, blazer badges, etc. A statuette of an East Lancashire soldier of 1916 is one of a set of five for sale.

In the extensive collection of medals in the museum, there are several which were awarded to men serving with the Pals.

CLITHEROE
North West Sound Archive, Steward's Office, Clitheroe Castle, Clitheroe, BB7 1AZ. Tel 01200 427897. Fax. 01200 427897

The Archive makes, collects and preserves sound recordings of the life, character, history and traditions of the north west of England. With over 85,000 recordings, it is probably the largest oral history collection in Great Britain outside London. Details of all recordings are held on computer. The Archive provides resource material and information for family history, local history and academic research, broadcasting, drama and schools.

Archive material relevant to the Pals consists of recorded interviews with ten veterans. These amount to approximately fourteen hours duration. The veterans describe a wide range of experiences from enlistment, training in England and Wales, service in Egypt. the Western Front and Army life in general.

MANCHESTER
North West Film Archive The Manchester Metropolitan University, Minshull House, 47 - 49 Chorlton Street, Manchester M1 3EU. Tel 0161 247 3097 Fax 0161 247 3098.

The Archive is Britain's largest public film collection outside London. It was set up in 1977 and is the professionally recognised home for films made in and about the north west. There are over 22,000 items dating from the 1890's to the present day. These include cinema newsreels, documentaries, etc. and professional and amateur productions ranging from corporate videos to home movies. Some 12,500 photographs, taped interviews and original documents are also held.

The Archive holds nineteen films relating to WW1. One, a newsreel, is *The Accrington Pals Battalion.* Made in 1915, it is in two parts; first, 'Marching at Salisbury' (Dec.), second, 'Marching at Accrington' (July). The running time is approximately five minutes.

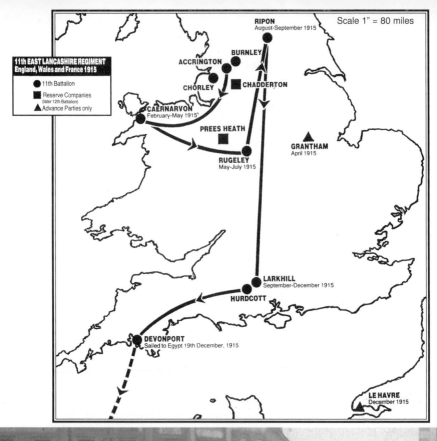

Scale 1" = 80 miles

RIPON
August-September 1915

BURNLEY

ACCRINGTON

CHORLEY

CHADDERTON

CAERNARVON
February-May 1915'

PREES HEATH

GRANTHAM
April 1915

RUGELEY
May-July 1915

LARKHILL
September-December 1915

HURDCOTT

DEVONPORT
Sailed to Egypt 19th December. 1915

LE HAVRE
December 1915

CHAPTER EIGHT

Camps and Billets in England and Wales – and Egypt

Introduction

When the Pals left their homes in February 1915 their good fortune, as far as home cooking was concerned, continued. Their first move was to Caernarfon, north Wales, and billets. The move to Rugeley Camp, Staffordshire, brought home to them the hard facts of barrack-room life and Army cooking. This continued at South Camp, Ripon, North Yorkshire, and finally, in England, at Hurdcott Camp, Wiltshire. In Egypt there was, of course, a complete contrast in both weather and accommodation.

Pte. Sayer's reminiscences in Chapter One help to convey a little of life in camp at that time. A look round the camp sites in the 1990s, however, gives no indication that here was 'home' for thousands of troops. Each has reverted to heathland or meadowland, with nothing, only a few pot shards or buckles etc. to mark the place. Only the towns have changed.

The Battalion stands at ease in Castle Square (Y Maes) Caernarfon in March 1915. *(The Pals Collection)*

CAERNARFON

Caernarfon (in 1915 Carnarvon) was the county town of Carnarvonshire, north Wales, until 1974 when it became the county town of Gwynedd.

Caernarfon is one of the few towns in the country which retains its medieval walls intact. The town is dominated by the Castle, built by Edward 1 (1239-1307) after the defeat and death of the last native prince of Wales, Llewelyn ap Gruffyd, in 1282. The castle was the scene of the investiture in 1301 of Edward's son (Edward II

159

1284-1327) as Prince of Wales. In 1911 the future Edward VIII became the new Prince. 1969 saw the investiture of Charles, the present Prince of Wales.

During their three months stay in Caernarfon in 1915 the Pals paraded every morning on Castle Square (Y Maes). The square was originally Castle Green, the site of a smaller Norman structure and, since 1284, the home of the weekly market.

In the square is the statue of the Rt. Hon. David Lloyd George, Liberal M.P. for Caernarfon from 1890 to 1945. He was the raiser of the Welsh Army Corps in 1914, many of whom were stationed in the neighbouring townships along the coast. In 1915 he became Minister for Munitions and he held office as Prime Minister from 1916 to 1922.

Throughout the 19th century Caernarfon's prosperity depended on the quarrying and shipment of roofing and writing (school) slates. Timber was imported and there was some fishing and coastal trade. At the end of the century, however, the slate industry declined and severe unemployment resulted. The population of the town went from 11,521 in 1891 to 9,119 in 1911 as people left the area.

The Pals came to Caernarfon on 23 February 1915 and left on 13 May. The officers mess was in the Royal (now Royal Celtic) Hotel on Bangor Street. Over 1,300 N.C.O.s and men were billeted in small hotels, boarding houses and private homes throughout the town. Many men were pleased they were placed in the town centre shops - "We were young and always hungry, it was nice to eat free cakes"

In this way the townspeople gained a much needed income and the Pals, who developed a friendly social relationship with the town, enjoyed their stay. For these reasons the stay seemed a short one and town and troops were sorry to part.

Although the population is almost unchanged from that of 1911 at 9,681 (1991 census) and unemployment is still high, present-day Caernarfon is a busy town. It is a market town and a major tourism centre. It is one of the most Welsh of towns, with some 70% of the population speaking Welsh as a first language. As the county town of Gwynedd it is the home of the County Council offices and it is also a major local commercial, financial and service industries centre for the county.

Only a small minority of people work in manufacturing i.e. in the clothing and automotive parts industries. Caernarfon, however, has a central part in the media industry with a TV film making unit and equipment supplier to the Welsh independent TV organisation - one of only two in Wales.

Next to this high technology, Caernarfon's medieval street lines behind the town walls are unchanged. Many of the buildings the Pals lived in or passed every day are still there. Coed Helen, their training ground across the River Seiont, would look just the same to them, except perhaps for the golf club and parts of the recreation ground.

During their stay many of the Pals did sentry duty in the Castle – 'We watched for German submarines in the Menai Straits'. Today, the Castle, acknowledged as one of the finest medieval castles in Europe, now attracts visitors from all over the world. The Castle is also the home of the regimental museum of the Royal Welsh Fusiliers, Wales' oldest regiment.

A 'Caernarfon Partnership' of Town and County Councils, the Tourist Board and the Welsh Development Agency, are working together to enhance the local economy and promote Caernarfon even more as a tourist centre. In 1915 the Pals enjoyed their stay in the town. In present times it is tourists from all over the world who enjoy Caernarfon.

There is no information about the Pals in Caernarfon Library. Contemporary issues of the Carnarvon and Denbigh Herald are on micro-film at the Caernarfon Area Record Office at Victoria Dock.

Sources:

A Visitors Guide to Caernarfon (Caernarfon Chamber of Trade).

Caernarfon Town Trail (Gwynedd County Council).

Staff at Caernarfon Library.

Staff at Caernarfon Castle.

RUGELEY

Rugeley is a market town on the edge of Cannock Chase in Staffordshire. It is ten miles from Stafford, eight from Lichfield and six from Cannock.

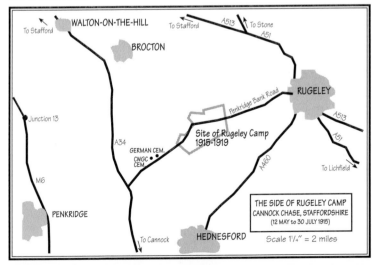

Part of Rugeley Camp in 1916. Note the railway line. *(Mr C J Whitehouse)*

The scene in 1998.
(The Author)

Cannock Chase is in origin a royal hunting forest created by William the Conquerer. It is a 17,000 acre (26 square miles) area of outstanding natural beauty. The Chase's forests and open heathland are the habitat for a great variety of wildlife, from rare insects to herds of fallow deer. The Cannock Chase Country Park is 3,000 acres (4.5 square miles) in extent, which makes it one of the largest country parks in Britain.

In the winter of 1914 and early 1915 two hutted camps, each to accommodate a full division, were hastily erected on the Chase near Rugeley and the village of Brocton. When the Pals arrived at Rugeley Camp (also known as Penkridge Bank Camp) in May 1915 many of the huts were not complete. Windows, doors, even roofs, were missing. Some 800 civilian workmen were on site erecting what was to be a total of 500 huts of all shapes and sizes - the Y.M.C.A. hut (which opened just before the Pals left for Ripon) was, for example, 188 feet long by 30 feet wide.

Some in Rugeley town were unhappy at what was being done to Cannock Chase. They found it difficult to believe that the sight of 'ugly wooden buildings of depressing uniformity' would give anyone pleasure. The Pals , and those who followed them, would have agreed.

In time, however, many existing roads were improved and over three miles of new roads were constructed. Each camp also had its own water, electricity and sewerage systems.

Rugeley is an ancient place. The Domesday Book of 1086 recorded nine villeins or small farmers living there. In 1259 the growing town was granted its weekly market charter. Rugeley was known for iron-working as early as 1231 and coal was mined in 1498. It developed into a thriving market town with one of the largest 'Horse Fairs' in the country.

By the early nineteenth century the construction of canals and railways transformed the agricultural economy of the town into one of coal mining, iron works and tanning. By 1911 the population was 7,189 and most were employed in those industries.

Today Rugeley is much changed. A pedestrianised area, car parks and supermarkets are the main features of the town centre. Returning Pals would however, still recognise the clock-tower and entrance - all that remains - of the Victorian Market Hall. It now serves as a health food store. Other buildings around the area (Horse Fair) also survive, notably the Globe Inn.

Post-war housing for Birmingham's overspill population helped to treble Rugeley's 1911 population to 23,505 in 1991. The coal mines, iron works and the tanneries are now gone. In their place nationally known firms make such as earth-moving machinery, electronic products and outdoor and sports clothing. The power station, which dominates the northern edge of the town, has (in 1998) an uncertain future as heavy industry in the area further declines.

Cannock Chase is also much changed from the days of 1914-1918. The Pals were one of the first battalions to arrive on the Chase, but by the end of the war almost a quarter of a million men passed through the camps. By now, of course, a relative peace and quiet has returned to the forests and heathlands. Penkridge Bank Road, from Rugeley, along which many a soldier trudged his way back to camp, is now a fairly wide, and busy, tarmac road. At the point where the camp began are now caravan sites with names such as 'Silvertrees' and 'Tackeroo'.

There is now a 'Museum of Cannock Chase' in nearby Hednesford. Cannock Chase Country Park has a Visitor Centre on Marquis Drive, on the site of the former R.A.F. 'Hednesford' 1939 - 1945 War training camp which closed in the 1960's. Details of way-marked trails, including a 'Great War Motor and Foot Trail' are available from both places. Near the Visitor Centre is the C.W.G.C. Cannock Chase War

Cemetery where some 375 servicemen of both wars are buried. Next to it is the final resting place of 4,941 German servicemen of both wars who died on British soil. This cemetery is also cared for by the Commonwealth War Graves Commission.

There is no specific information about the Pals in Rugeley Library. In Cannock Library Local Studies Department there is a file of newspaper cuttings and photographs which gives much information about the construction and use of all the camps on Cannock Chase.

Sources:

Rugeley Official Town Guide

'A Town for Four Winters' by C. J. Whitehouse

Staff at Rugeley and Cannock Libraries

Staff at The Museum of Cannock Chase'.

RIPON

The city of Ripon, North Yorkshire, grew gradually from the church and monastery established by St. Wilfred in about 670 A.D. Ripon Cathedral is one of Britain's oldest Christian buildings.

In the Middle Ages, Ripon's prosperity was based on the woollen trade and leather making. In the 17th and 18th century the city was famous for the manufacture, and quality, of spurs. The early 18th century also saw the beginnings of the racecourse on Ripon Common and a temporary popularity as a spa.

The Industrial Revolution however, passed Ripon by, so by the end of the 19th century the only industry was paint and varnish manufacturing and some iron making. The main role of the city was as

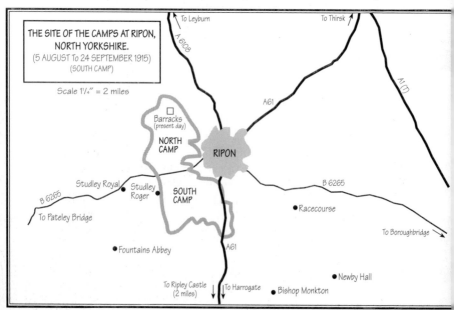

THE SITE OF THE CAMPS AT RIPON, NORTH YORKSHIRE.
(5 AUGUST To 24 SEPTEMBER 1915)
(SOUTH CAMP)

Scale 1¼" = 2 miles

the market and trading centre for the surrounding agricultural area. In the early years of the 20th century Ripon City Council, in an effort to bring in extra income, requested the War Office to station troops in the city. They were refused.

In December 1914 came a dramatic and welcome change. The War Office decided that Ripon, its population 7,000, would become a training centre for over 30,000 troops. On hearing the news the then Mayor lamented that 'The old-worldliness and charm of Ripon will be a thing of the past'. 3,000 navvies and joiners built two camps in three months. In time 'North' and 'South' Camps, as they were known, had hundreds of barrack rooms, a power station, canteens, theatres, cinemas, a hospital and a post office. There were miles of water, sewerage and electricity systems, twenty-six miles of roads and a narrow-gauge railway running through the area. The village of Studley Roger was almost encircled by South Camp.

The Pals were at South Camp from 5 August to 24 September 1915, whilst they took their musketry course. Unfortunately, no records of the camp seem to have survived and few physical traces remain. In 1940 barracks were again built on part of the site to house

The scene in 1998.
(The Author)

Part of the market square, Ripon in 1914.
(Ripon Tourist Information Centre)

the Royal Engineers School of Military Engineering, transferred from Chatham (to which they returned in 1948). (The Royal Engineers still have a barracks on the site and retain a strong association with the city).

Only a few local placenames e.g. 'Hospital Wood', now give a clue to what was once a complete township. Most of the area not reclaimed for agriculture is now used for recreational land, residential development and small industrial estates.

The effect of the camp on Ripon was startling to say the least. The city did get its extra income as the Pals, and in time, many others, spent their pay in the shops, cafes and public houses. It was inevitable that Ripon mothers issued the age-old warning to daughters – 'Get yourself into trouble and you're in that work-house'. Most memories of Ripon however, were of tea and cakes in the cafes on the Market Square, the Hornblower sounding his horn at nine p.m., the Unicorn public house (officers only) and attending church parade at the Cathedral.

At the present time all these things can still be seen and done. Every evening the Hornblower 'sets the watch' in the Market Square, continuing a tradition dating from medieval times.

The present population of Ripon, at 13,866, is double that of 1914. The city has lost none of its charm, in spite of the 1914 Mayor's lament. It is still a busy market town, but its workforce is now mainly (67%) in the service industries of distribution, catering and banking etc. Agricultural machinery is made and repaired and there are several light engineering works.

As 'Yorkshire's Cathedral City of the Dales' Ripon is a popular centre for tourists. The 'Tourist Trail' around the city includes, at 24 Borrage Lane, the cottage where Wilfred Owen spent a brief period of

The memorial on the site of the Catholic Women's League Chapel and Canteen, near Studley Roger. *(The Author)*

THIS SHRINE WAS ERECTED IN 1921
ON THE SITE OF THEIR CHAPEL AND CANTEE
BY THE CATHOLIC WOMEN'S LEAGUE OF
THE LEEDS DIOCESE
IN MEMORY OF THE BRITISH AND CANADIAN
SERVICEMEN OF RIPON CAMP
WHO GAVE THEIR LIVES IN THE GREAT WAR 1914-
IT ALSO COMMEMORATES THEIR SUCCESSORS
WHO DIED IN WORLD WAR TWO 1939-1945

MAY THEY REST IN PEACE

convalescence in 1918. Outside the city, on the B625, near the village of Studley Roger, is a memorial to those men stationed at North and South Camps who later lost their lives in the war. The memorial faces the site of North Camp hospital. Behind the memorial is the site of the Catholic Women's League chapel and canteen.

In the city centre, road signs and traffic congestion apart, the Market Square today would still be instantly recognisable to the shades of any Pals returning.

There is no specific information about the Pals in Ripon Library. There is however, a 'Military' file containing references to North and South Camps.

Sources:

'About Historic Ripon', published by Ripon Civic Society

Staff at Ripon and Harrogate Libraries

Staff at Ripon Tourist Information Centre.

HURDCOTT

Hurdcott in south Wiltshire is not a village. The name on the Ordnance Survey map indicates Hurdcott House (built 1631, enlarged 1901). Within its extensive grounds is a 'Home Farm' with stables and several cottages for the estate workers. Neither were the Pals on Salisbury Plain as such. Hurdcott is in the valley of the River Nadder, which rises near Shaftesbury, to the south of the Plain, and flows eighteen miles to the River Avon at Salisbury.

To begin at the beginning. After the Army learned hard lessons in markmanship and mobility in the first Boer War in 1881, it was apparent that the formal manoeuvres at Aldershot were going to be

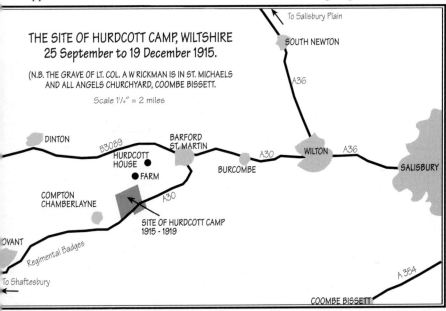

THE SITE OF HURDCOTT CAMP, WILTSHIRE
25 September to 19 December 1915.

(N.B. THE GRAVE OF LT. COL. A W RICKMAN IS IN ST. MICHAELS AND ALL ANGELS CHURCHYARD, COOMBE BISSETT.

Scale 1¼" = 2 miles

The former south entrance to Hurdcott Camp, part of the camp was in the field beyond. *(The Author)*

rehearsals for more disasters. Salisbury Plain, with its open, rolling, downs, was a ready-made training area. By 1902 the War Office had acquired the estates of Bulford, Tidworth, Durrington and Larkhill – a total of some 43,500 acres. (The total area is now some 92,000 acres).

With the outbreak of war in 1914 hutted and tented camps sprang up all over the Plain. They eventually overflowed into the valleys of the Rivers Wylye and Nadder. In 1915 work began on a hutted camp at Hurdcott in the Nadder Valley. The Pals arrived there from Ripon in September 1915 and, apart from a short stay at Larkhill Camp, were there until 19 December 1915 when they left for Egypt.

The site of Hurdcott Camp is by the Wilton to Shaftesbury road (the A30) between Barford St. Martin and Compton Chamberlayne. Barford St. Martin is a large village where the A30 turns sharply over a narrow bridge. Housing developments since the 1960's have changed it into a commuter village for Salisbury, six miles away. Fortunately the village has not become suburban in character. The thatched cottages, the inn and the church around the crossroads in the centre are much as they were in 1915.

The A30 passes along the valley of the River Nadder, perhaps one of the most beautiful of Wiltshire's valleys. It is a rich mixture of small stone villages and rolling downlands with occasional woods and copses. At a later date parts of the Somme were to remind the Pals of the area.

The south entrance to Hurdcott House and farm is just over a mile from Barford St. Martin. It is a quiet, isolated, spot. A further mile beyond is the hamlet of Compton Chamberlayne – its beautiful parkland setting second to none in the valley. Across the road from the south entrance is a large dilapidated hut. The hut, a former guardroom, was used until recently to house tractors and farm machinery until it became too dangerous. It survives because it was home for a local family for many years after the war.

The site of the camp, on both sides of the road, is now all cultivated fields. A car sales centre at Little Heath, by the A30, marks the end of the camp area. Not a trace of the camp can be seen. When the war ended the huts were dismantled, the concrete bases broken up and the land put back to the plough. Occasionally pot shards and other debris are seen by farm workers. Pheasants and rabbits may be glimpsed in the woods between the road and the farm (the woods were out of bounds in 1915 - a point ignored by the poachers of the Battalion). Only the sound of passing traffic now spoils the tranquillity.

After the Pals left, Hurdcott was used by Australian troops. In March 1917 Hurdcott House became the headquarters of No. 3 Command of the Australian Imperial Forces. It was 1920 before the

Below is the postcard sent by Sgt Rigby to his wife and children, it reads: 'X denotes which way we came on the Plain after an 18 mile march. See them things in the sky, there are plenty of them here, everytime you look up you can see a dozen'.
Left is the same scene taken in 1998.

house was restored to the owners.

The Australians, and other troops in the valley, left their mark in the form of regimental badges cut into the chalky hillside near Fovant, three miles beyond Hurdcott. (The Fovant Regimental Badge Society holds its meetings in the Pembroke Arms, Fovant)

The Nadder Valley is rich in history. Wilton, a four mile walk on the Salisbury road for the Pals, was a borough with its own mint before the Kingdom of England existed. Alfred the Great defeated the Danes here in 871 A.D. Three miles further is Salisbury, a medieval city with many attractions ranging from old inns and river walks to the magnificent cathedral, completed in 1258.

Before and since those times the River Nadder ran through a peaceful rural valley. Only in 1914 to 1918 was the peace disrupted by so many thousands of troops. Of these, only the Fovant badges remain.

Sources:

'Wiltshire Villages' by Brian Woodruffe, publ. Robert Hale 1982

Staff at Salisbury Library

Staff at Salisbury Tourist Information Centre

EGYPT

Most present-day visitors to Egypt arrive by air at Cairo, the capital city. The lure of ancient Egypt and the River Nile – the Pyramids, Abu Simbel and the Valley of the Kings, etc. – is so great that few tourists see much of the isthmus of Suez and the Canal.

In the past many visitors to Egypt were simply passing through the Suez Canal. It was the custom to disembark at either Alexandria or Port Said, race to see the Pyramids, then race back to the ship as it reached the other end of the Canal. Today, tourists arriving by sea are usually on cruise liners whose itinerary includes a 'stop-over' at Port Said for a day's excursion to Cairo and the Pyramids. The towns on the Canal banks are rarely on the list of 'places to see'.

The lure of ancient Egypt is understandable. It is a country with a long, unbroken history. Over 4,000 years before the birth of Christ, Egypt was one of the most advanced and civilised countries in the world. There was an established Egyptian state in 3,100 B.C. The country was ruled for almost 2,800 years by a total of thirty-one Pharaonic dynasties. It was during their reign the Pyramids at Giza and the awesome temples and antiquities of Abu Simbel, Karnak and Luxor, amongst many others, were built.

The first canal in the region seems to have been dug about 1850 B.C. In 521 B.C. there was a canal from Cairo to Suez. A few centuries

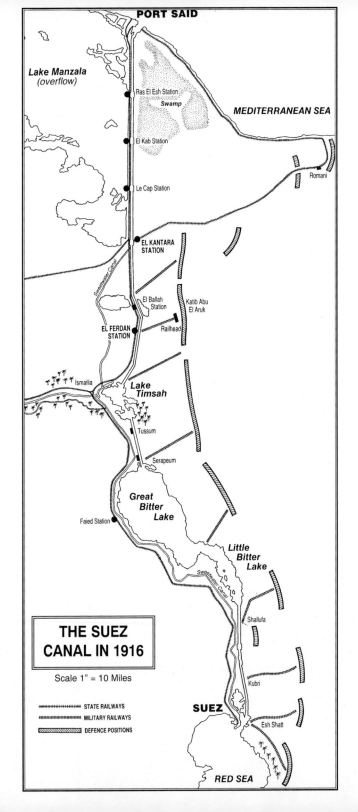

PORT SAID

Lake Manzala
(overflow)

MEDITERRANEAN SEA

Ras El Esh Station
Swamp

El Kab Station

Romani

Le Cap Station

EL KANTARA
STATION

El Ballah
Station

Katib Abu
El Aruk

EL FERDAN
STATION

Railhead

Ismailia

Lake
Timsah

Tussum

Serapeum

*Great
Bitter
Lake*

*Little
Bitter
Lake*

Faied Station

Shallufa

Kubri

THE SUEZ
CANAL IN 1916

Scale 1" = 10 Miles

Esh Shatt

SUEZ

STATE RAILWAYS
MILITARY RAILWAYS
DEFENCE POSITIONS

RED SEA

later, after the Romans departed, the canal was allowed to silt up. In 1854 Sa'id Pasha, the Khedive of Egypt, granted Ferdinand de Lesseps the right to build a canal from Port Said to Suez. It was completed in 1869.

In 1914 Britain declared Egypt a Protectorate. From then on the country became a huge concentration of British, Australian and other Imperial troops. Preparations for the campaigns in Gallipoli and Palestine brought about heavy demands by the military on the civilian population for native labour, transport, buildings and the purchase or requisition of animals, etc.

The Suez Canal, particularly after a Turkish attack in 1915, became a front-line of defence. To assist in the defence of the Canal a light railway was constructed into the Sinai Desert. (One starting point was the small Canal town of El Kantara, which was to become the biggest military city in the world at that time - as it was in the 1939-1945 War).

The Pals disembarked at Port Said on 5 January 1916 and left Port Said for Marseilles on 2 March 1916. The Pal's duties in Egypt were mainly piquet patrols, escorting ships en-route from Port Said to Suez, operating a chain ferry at El Ferdan and constructing the light railway from El Kantara.

In 1916 Port Said, at the northern end, and Suez, at the southern end of the Suez Canal, were 'company ' towns, centred on trade and administration. Although both had their squalid areas with native shops and bazaars, there were also many villas in tree-lined squares and on quiet boulevards dating from De Lesseps time. Those Pals who were

A group of Officers relax in the sun at El Ferdan. *(The Pals Collection)*

Port Said War Memorial Cemetery. Two of the Pals who died during the Battalion's two month stay are buried here. *(C.W.G.C.)*

able dined in the evenings at cafes to the accompaniment of a trio playing the latest tunes from home.

A Pal looking to do the same today would not recognise either town. Port Said, as a Canal city – 'The Gateway to the East' – is a flourishing city of some half a million inhabitants. It has now completely recovered from the damage caused by Israeli shells and bombs in the wars of 1967 and 1973. It still has tree-lined squares and boulevards but now there are also blocks of apartments and fine shops. Port Said has also large industrial zones complete with oil refineries, chemical works and huge warehouses. Its harbours and docks bustle with Canal traffic and the city also prospers because of its 'duty free' zone for shoppers. A famous landmark, in 1916 and the present day, is the Suez Canal Building, a gleaming white two storey building with three brilliant green domes.

The town of Suez, if anything, was even more affected by the wars with Israel. Three-quarters of the town was razed to the ground and the whole town evacuated. Now re-built, and with a population of 458,000, Suez is now an industrial centre producing cement, fertiliser and petro-chemicals.

Motorways and modern railways now run the length of the Canal. Modern Tunnels and under-passes carry road and rail to the eastern, Sinai side. A free passenger ferry has, however, replaced the chain ferry at El Ferdan which the Pals helped to operate in February 1916 (see Pte. Sayer's description, Chapter One). Another underpass is at El

Kantara, where the Pals worked on the military light railway (El Kantara suffered even more damage in the 1967 and 1973 wars and became a ghost town. The building of the underpass helped to revitalise the town).

In 1916 some of the Pals learned to swim in the Canal - the most able 'swam to Africa and back'. There are now several swimming clubs, with refreshments, a sandy beach and, if one dodges the passing supertankers, an opportunity to swim to either Asia or Africa and back. The present day swim is longer. In recent years the Suez Canal has been considerably widened and deepened to accommodate ships displacing up to a quarter of a million tons – ten times the weight of most ships of 1916.

This emphasises the difference between Egypt and the Suez Canal today from the time of the Pals. At that time Egypt was a desperately poor country depending on agriculture and yet hardly able to feed itself. Egypt, with double the population at almost sixty million people, now has major manufacturing industries such as steel production, petroleum, chemical products, motor cars and textiles. Egypt is also one of the world's main producers of raw cotton. Of all the places the Pals saw in the war, with the possible exception of the pulverised villages on the Western Front, Egypt has changed the most.

N.B. Place names have also changed. The present day names of the main places mentioned are:- Bur Sa'id (Port Said); El Suweis (Suez); Al-Qantarah (El Kantara) and Al - Firdan (El Ferdan).
Sources:
Fodor's Guide to Egypt 1996
Egypt Handbook, Moon Publ. 1995

CEMETERIES, MEMORIALS AND MEN

The battalion which was almost destroyed before Serre on 1 July 1916 rose again to continue to fight, with honour, throughout 1917 and 1918.

The complete nominal roll, and medal returns, of the Battalion totals more than 3,600 names. This is over three times the number of 'original Pals' who enlisted in September 1914. This illustrates more than anything else the rate at which casualties and transfers etc. were replaced during four years of war

At least 846 Pals and former Pals died on active service. Of these 471 lie in graves in 101 different cemeteries scattered throughout northern France and in Belgium. A total of 318 are commemorated on seven memorials. Others, including Pals transferred to other East Lancashire Regiment battalions or to other regiments for a variety of reasons, lie in Iraq, Egypt and Greece. Prisoners of war are buried in Germany and Holland.

It could be said that 846 is a minimal number. The number of those who died after the war, because of wounds or the effects of gas etc. is, of course, unknown. This 'death rate' continued even into the 1960's. All these men were buried in private, family, graves.

The following lists state (Part One) the cemeteries in which Pals and ex-Pals are buried. Each cemetery is in alphabetical order and numbered accordingly. The total numbers of burials in each is also shown. Memorials shown by an initial letter.

Part Two lists each soldier's name together with a letter or number to indicate the cemetery or memorial.

The symbols used on the maps are:
- ■ Cemetery where a Pal is buried
- □ Cemetery where an 'original' Pal is buried
- ▲ Memorial listing a Pal
- △ Memorial listing an 'original' Pal

A temporary war graves cemetery. *(Taylor Library)*

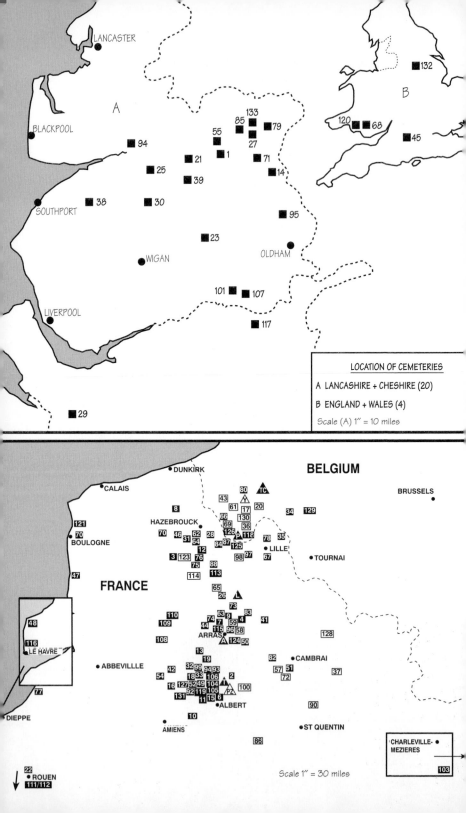

LANCASTER

A

BLACKPOOL

■ 94

■ 25
■ 21 ■ 1
■ 39

SOUTHPORT ■ 38 ■ 30

■ 23

WIGAN

LIVERPOOL

■ 29

B

■ 132

■ 120 ■ 68
■ 45

■ 85 ■ 133
■ 55 ■ 79
■ 27
■ 71
■ 14

■ 95

OLDHAM

■ 101 ■ 107

■ 117

LOCATION OF CEMETERIES

A LANCASHIRE + CHESHIRE (20)

B ENGLAND + WALES (4)

Scale (A) 1″ = 10 miles

DUNKIRK **BELGIUM**

CALAIS BRUSSELS

80
43 ▲ 1C
61 17 20
66 130 34 129
HAZEBROUCK 69 36
70 46 31 28 126 87 118 78 35
62 64 84 125 67 LILLE
121 3 123 76 12 98 97 TOURNAI
70 75
BOULOGNE 88
114 113

FRANCE

47 65
26 ▲
73
110 53 7 83
48 109 74 59 41
44 115 96 58
116 108 ARRAS ▲ 124 50 128
LE HAVRE 13
19 82 CAMBRAI
42 32 99 93 57 51
54 106 72 37
77 16 127 49 104 2
131 92 119 105 ▲ P2 100
15 6 90
11 ●ALBERT
DIEPPE 10
AMIENS ●ST QUENTIN
86

CHARLEVILLE-
MEZIERES ●
→
103

22
●ROUEN
111/112

Scale 1″ = 30 miles

PART ONE – THE CEMETERIES AND MEMORIALS
CEMETERIES

No.		Graves
1	Accrington Cemetery	8
2	Achiet-le-Grand Communal Cemetery Extension	2
3	Aire Communal Cemetery	1
4	Albuera Cemetery, Bailleul-sire-Berthoult	13
5	Amara War Cemetery	3
6	Ancre British Cemetery, Beaumont Hamel	1
7	Anzin-St. Aubin British Cemetery	1
8	Arneke British Cemetery	1
9	Arras Road British Cemetery, Roclincourt	6
10	Aubigny Communal Cemetery	2
11	Auchonvillers Military Cemetery	3
12	Aval Wood Military Cemetery, Vieux-Berquin	45
13	Bac-du-sud British Cemetery, Bailleulval	1
14	Bacup (Fairwell) Cemetery	2
15	Beaumont Hamel British Cemetery	1
16	Beauval Communal Cemetery	4
17	Bedford House Enclosure No.4, Zillebeke	1
18	Bertrancourt Military Cemetery	13
19	Bienvillers Military Cemetery	1
20	Birr Crossroads Cemetery, Zillebeke	1
21	Blackburn Cemetery	4
22	Boisguillaume Communal Cemetery Extension, Rouen	3
23	Bolton (Heaton) Cemetery	1
24	Boulogne Eastern Cemetery	4
25	Brindle (St.James) Churchyard	1
26	Brown's Road Military Cemetery, Festubert	4
27	Burnley Cemetery	4
28	Caestre Military Cemetery	6
29	Chester General Cemetery	1
30	Chorley Cemetery	2
31	Cinq Rues British Cemetery, Hazebrouck	8
32	Couin British Cemetery	3
33	Courcelles-au-Bois Communal Cemetery Extension	1
34	Courtrai Communal Cemetery (St.Jean)	1
35	Cretinier Cemetery, Wattrelos	4
36	Croonaert Chapel Cemetery, Wytschaete	1
37	Crossroads Cemetery, Fontaine-au-Bois	1
38	Croston (St.Michael) Churchyard	2
39	Darwen Cemetery	3
40	Doiran Military Cemetery	1
41	Douai British Cemetery, Cuincy	1
42	Doullens Communal Cemetery, Extension No.1	5
43	Dozinghem Military Cemetery, Westvleteren	1
44	Duisans British Cemetery, Etrun	10
45	Durrington Cemetery, Amesbury	1
46	Ebblinghem Military Cemetery	3
47	Etaples Military Cemetery	6
48	Etretat Churchyard	1

177

49	Euston Road Cemetery, Colincamps	26
50	Feuchy Chapel British Cemetery, Wancourt	1
51	Flesquieres Hill British Cemetery	2
52	Forceville Communal Cemetery Extension	1
53	Gaza War Cemetery	1
54	Gezaincourt Communal Cemetery Extension	1
55	Great Harwood Cemetery	1
56	Heilly Station Cemetery, Mericourt-l'Abbe	1
57	Hermies Hill British Cemetery	1
58	Hevin Farm British Cemetery, St. Laurent-Blangy	1
59	Highland Cemetery, Roclincourt	1
60	Kirechoi-Hortakoi Military Cemetery	1
61	Klein Vierstraat British Cemetery, Kemmel	1
62	La Kreule Military Cemetery, Hazebrouck	8
63	La Targette British Cemetery (Aux Rietz)	6
64	Le Grand Hasard Military Cemetery	15
65	Le Touret Military Cemetery, Richebourg-l'Avoue	1
66	Lijssenthoek Military Cemetery, Poperinghe	2
67	Lille Southern Cemetery	3
68	Llanwynno (St. Gwynno) Churchyard	1
69	Locre Hospice Cemetery	1
70	Longuenesse Souvenir Cemetery, St. Omer	10
71	Loveclough Providence United Methodist Churchyard	1
72	Lowne Cemetery, Havrincourt	1
73	Maroc British Cemetery, Grenay	1
74	Maroeuil British Cemetery	1
75	Merville Communal Cemetery	4
76	Merville Communal Cemetery Extension	1
77	Mont Huon Military Cemetery, Le Treport	1
78	Mouvaix New Communal Cemetery	1
79	Nelson Cemetery	1
80	New Irish Farm Cemetery, St.J ean-les-Ypres	2
81	Niederzwehren Cemetery, Kassel	1
82	Ontario Cemetery, Sains-les-Marquion	1
83	Orchard Dump Cemetery, Arleux-en-Gohelle	1
84	Outtersteene Communal Cemetery Extension	13
85	Padiham Cemetery	2
86	Pargny British Cemetery	1
87	Pont-d'Achelles Military Cemetery, Nieppe	9
88	Pont-du-Hem Military Cemetery, La Gorgue	2
89	Port Said War Memorial Cemetery	2
90	Premont British Cemetery	1
91	Preston (New Hall Lane) Cemetery	2
92	Puchevillers British Cemetery	2
93	Queen's Cemetery, Puisieux	50
94	Railway Hollow Cemetery, Hebuterne	15
95	Rochdale Cemetery	1
96	Roclincourt Military Cemetery	11
97	Rue-Petillon Military Cemetery, Fleurbaix	1
98	Rue-du-Bois Military Cemetery, Fleurbaix	1
99	Sailly-au-Bois Military Cemetery	12
100	Sailly-Saillisel British Cemetery	1

101	Salford (Weaste) Cemetery	1
102	Salonika Anglo-French Cemetery, Lembet Road	1
103	Sedan (St. Charles) Communal Cemetery	3
104	Serre Road Cemetery, No.1, Hebuterne	1
105	Serre Road Cemetery, No.2, Beaumont Hamel	3
106	Serre Road Cemetery, No.3, Puisieux	6
107	Southern Cemetery, Manchester	1
108	St. Hilaire Cemetery, Frevent	3
109	St. Pol British Cemetery, St. Pol-sur-Ternoise	1
110	St. Pol Communal Cemetery Extension	2
111	St. Sever Cemetery Extension, Rouen	4
112	St. Sever Cemetery, Rouen	1
113	St. Vaast Post Military Cemetery, Richebourg l'Avou	11
114	St. Venant-Robeecq Road British Cemetery, Robecq	1
115	Ste. Catherine British Cemetery, Arras	3
116	Ste. Marie Cemetery, Le Havre	1
117	Stockport Cemetery	1
118	Srand Military Cemetery, Ploegsteert	5
119	Sucrerie Military Cemetery, Colincamps	4
120	Swansea Hebrew Congregation Cemetery	1
121	Terlincthun British Cemetery, Wimille	12
122	The Hague (Den Haag) General Cemetery	1
123	Thiennes British Cemetery	1
124	Tilloy British Cemetery, Tilloy-les-Mofflaines	1
125	Trois Arbres Cemetery, Steenwerck	10
126	Underhill Farm Cemetery, Ploegsteert	16
127	Varennes Military Cemetery	1
128	Vendegies Crossroads British Cemetery, Bermerain	1
129	Vichte Military Cemetery	3
130	Voormezeele Enclosure No. 3	1
131	Warloy-Baillon Communal Cemetery Extension	1
132	Wombwell Cemetery	1
133	Worsthorne Wesleyan Churchyard	1

PRIVATE BURIALS

134	Coombe Bissett (St. Michael &All Angels) Churchyard	1
135	Mitton (All Hallows) Churchyard	1
136	Moston (St. Joseph's) Cemetery	1
137	Oswaldtwistle (Immanuel) Baptist Churchyard	1
138	Rishton Cemetery	1

MEMORIALS

Ltr.	Name	Inscr.
A	Arras	84
B	Basra	1
H	Helles	1
L	Loos	3
P	Ploegsteert	70
PZ	Pozieres	4
T	Thiepval	145
TC	Tyne Cot	7
Y	Ypres	4

PART TWO – **THE MEN**

Adams, Albert Henry P
Ainsworth, Eli A
Ainsworth, Thomas 88
Allen, Albert 107
Allen, Thomas 99
Allen, William 106
Archer, William John 10
Arkwright, Robert V 85
Ashworth, Fred 93
Ashworth, Thomas A
Aspden, Albert A
Aspden, Austin Segar A
Aspin, George Alfred A
Aspin, Herbert T
Aspin, Thomas A
Aspinall, Harry 96
Aspinall, William PZ
Astin, Harry P
Astley, Robert 93
Atkinson, Arthur 63
Atkinson, James A
Atkinson, Stranger 87
Atkinson, Thomas 49
Auchterlonie, James 111

Bailey, Albert A
Bailey, William 26
Baines, John William 16
Baldwin, George A
Baldwin, Joseph A
Banks, Roland T
Barlow, Edmund 17
Barnes, George T
Barnes, George Worsick T
Barnes, James T
Barnes, Joseph T
Barnes, Wainright 122
Baron, William 89
Barrett, William 113
Barton, James A

Bate, William 121
Bateman, Walter L
Bateson, Thomas A
Batley, George Alexander 44
Baxter, Richard 93
Beacall, Arthur 49
Beaghan, David T
Beaumont, George Joseph 127
Beetham, T.E. 91
Bell, Albert A
Bell, Joseph T
Bell, William P
Bentley, Oswald A
Berry, Robert 13
Berry, Thomas T
Best, Joseph W P
Best, William TC
Beswick, Charles 125
Bibby, Arthur A
Bibby, Henry 32
Billington, Joshua 12
Billington, Walter Cyril 94
Bird, Frederick A
Birtwistle, John W 64
Birtwistle, Richard P
Blackstone, John 49
Blackwell, Reginald 12
Blake, Reginald J A P
Blakey, Frederick 93
Boden, William 133
Bolton, James Isherwood 121
Bolton, John Albert 4
Bolton, William 93
Booth, Frederick 47
Booth, George P
Booth, George William 132
Booth, J 51
Boothman, Joseph A
Bottomley, Leslie Vincent 12
Bowden, Harry TC
Bowers, Walter T

Bowers, William T
Bowling, John 47
Boyle, James 99
Bracewell, Frederick W 49
Braddock, William 67
Bradley, William Henry 55
Bradshaw, Tom 28
Brady, Daniel 70
Breckell, George Edwin T
Brennan, Edmund B 46
Brennan, James 63
Brennand, Arthur 96
Bretherton, William T
Briddon, Benjamin S P
Brierley, John 21
Briggs, Robert 49
Briggs, Walter T
Brindle, Francis T
Broadbent, Frank 63
Broadley, Fred T
Broadley, Thomas Y
Brooke, Herbert 75
Brooks, John T, 108
Brotherton, John F 46
Brown, Birkett 99
Brown, Sidney Wilfrid P
Brown, William A
Browne, James L 101
Brumwell, Albert C 64
Brunskill, Arthur 49
Bryan, Percy A
Buckley, Arthur 96
Buckley, Frederick 96
Bullen, Robert 85
Burgess, Henry P
Burrows, James Richard 32
Burt, Charles Edgar P
Burt, Harold Reginald A
Bury, Albert T
Bury, J 39
Bury, Percy T

Butterfield, Richard 12
Butterworth, Jordan A

Calderbank, Henry Y
Calvert, Jack T
Camm, Fred T
Carey, Thomas T
Carr, William T
Carter, Harry P
Caseley, William J G A
Cassidy, Francis 113
Catterall, John A
Chadwick, Edward 94
Chamberlain, Walter 12
Chapman, Harry T
Chapman, William T, 47
Charnley, Robert T
Chrimes, Thomas 99
Christopher, John Henry 87
Clapham, Henry A
Clapham, John M T
Clark, Charles T
Clark, Jack 119
Clark, Samuel Walter A
Clarke, Leonard William 52
Clarke, Thomas Henry 126
Clarkson, William 49
Claypole, Charles L P
Clayton, George T
Clayton, Herbert 49
Clegg, William T
Clements, Arthur John 12
Cliffe, Arthur 50
Cliffe, Bernard 18
Clifford, Thomas Jeffrey 121
Clinton, Harry T
Clough, Thomas 40
Coady, Thomas 93
Coates, James T
Cohen, Oscar 120
Coleman, Bernard 28

Coleman, Richard A P
Collier, George 115
Collinge, Harry P
Connor, Harry 64
Connor, John 5
Conroy, Thomas 70
Conway, Arthur P 93
Cook, Thomas 93
Cook, William T
Cooper, Harry P
Cork, William Rennie 12
Cosgrove, Michael P
Coulthard, Richard 19
Courtney, John 87
Cowburn, Harry P
Cowell, John William T
Cowgill, Albert 115
Cox , Charles 93
Coyne, Michael 7
Crabtree, Samuel A
Crankshaw, Ernest P
Crawshaw, George W 99
Creer, Edward 121
Cronkshaw, Haworth 99
Cronshaw, Thomas Edgar 6
Cropper, J 121
Cross, Arthur T
Cross, Richard 47
Cullen, Michael T
Cunliffe, John 93
Cunliffe, William J 96
Cutler, Ernest 43

Darlington, John PZ
Davies, Harry Noel T
Davies, Henry P
Davies, John Henry T
Davies, Robert James 126
Davis, Eric 118
Davis, John Thomas 93
Davison, James 115

Dawson, Oscar 49
Dean, Harold P
Dean, Herbert 12
Delaney, Thomas T
Dempsey, Patrick 57
Denney, John 106
Dent, Arthur 124
Dewhurst, Harry 61
Dewhurst, Thomas P
Dewhurst, William 84
Dickinson, George Alfred 129
Dickinson, James T
Dickinson, Robin 103
Dix, Alfred Boon 93
Dixon, Harry 93
Dixon, Robert P
Dorning, Harry 117
Dougherty, William T
Downes, Alfred 18
Driver, John A
Duckett, John TC
Duckworth, Thomas H 99
Duckworth, William 18
Duerden, Orrell T T
Duffell, Ernest Alfred TC
Duncan, Frederick A P
Dunn, Walter Stuart 44
Dust, Thomas Frank 94

Earnshaw, Joseph A 67   ·
Eastham, John 121
Eccles, James 62
Eddy, Charles Ritchie A
Edge, Israel 93
Edwards, Alfred 49
Edwards, William A
Ellison, Wilfred 16
Emmett, James H 93
Enderby, Joseph T
Entwistle, Carswell T
Entwistle, John A

Evans, Alfred Henry C 45
Evans, Brian A

Fadden, Michael 59
Fawcett, Frank 18
Fell, Edgar 96
Fielding, James William 126
Fielding, John 96
Fielding, William T 24
Finney, William T
Finnigan, Joseph 12
Firth, John 87
Firth, Wilfred P
Fishwick, William Alfred 87
Fitzgerald, Albert E P
Fletcher, Peter 110
Fogg, Robert 4
Foreman, Arthur 12
Foster, Philip 35
Francis, Thomas Edward T
Fullelove, William 84
Fuller, Thomas Dyson 125
Fuller, William 28

Gallagher, John P 62
Gardner, George A
Gaskell, Thomas 110, 23
Gelling, James 35
George, John Ieuan 64
Gibbens, Sydney H 93
Gibson, Albert T
Godfrey, Albert 44
Goodfellow, Sydney 64
Goodier, Ernest 131
Goodwin, Harold A
Gotts, Clarence Augustus A
Green, James 4
Green, John 12
Green, Robert 74
Green, William T, 126
Greenhalgh, William P

Greenwood, Fred T
Greenwood, William 22
Gresty, James TC
Grimshaw, Henry 73
Grimshaw, Joseph T
Grimshaw, Thomas 93
Grimshaw, Walter 35
Grimshaw, William T
Grindrod, James Henry P
Grue, Henry 51

Hacking, Frederick 137
Hacking, Percy T 1
Haddock, Charles 64
Haigh, Reginald 94
Halewood, George L T
Hall, Herbert 62
Hall, John 125
Halliwell, Arthur 31
Halstead, Albert 49
Halstead, Charles A
Halstead, Edward 113
Hanley, John 96
Hardman, Harry 49
Hardman, Samuel Davies 93
Hardy, Ernest 62
Hargreaves, Albert 93
Hargreaves, Frederick A, 103
Hargreaves, James 113
Hargreaves, Joseph 125
Hargreaves, Percy 54
Harling, Charles 1
Harradine, Bertram 96
Harris, Percival Samuel 126
Harrison, Henry B T
Harrison, Stephen A, 21
Hart, Alfred 94
Hart, James 72
Hartley, Alan A
Hartley, Albert 113
Hartley, Benjamin 44

Ingham, Harry 94
Ingham, Lawrence P
Ingham, Richard 94
Inman, R H 12
Irvine, Andrew 49
Irving, Edward P
Isherwood, Joseph 69
Ithell, John William 121

Jackson, Arthur T
Jackson, James T
Jackson, Robert 93
Jackson, Thomas H 119
Jagger, Archer A
James, Richard Walter 4
Johns, Thomas George P
Johnson, Robert 125
Johnstone, Peter James 129
Jolly, David 42
Jones, George A
Jones, Herbert 9
Jones, Norman T
Jones, Thomas Edward 12
Jordan, James Douglas T
Joys, James William 75

Kearnes, Frederick 82
Kellett, Peter 108
Kennedy, Thomas 93
Kenworthy, Albert W T
Kenyon, Ernest 18
Kenyon, George 9
Kirby, George 84
Kirkham, Charles Arthur 24
Kitchen, Wilfrid 12
Knapper, Arthur 12
Kneen, William E 129
Knighton, John 70
Knowles, James T
Knowles, William 99
Kohn, Wilfred Arthur 49

Lacey, Cornelius P
Laffy, John T
Lambert, Thomas 93
Lambert, William M 64
Lancaster, James L
Lane, Cornelius 128
Lane, William Ewart 31
Lang, Austin T
Last, H E 44
Lawrenson, John 16
Lawton, Ebenezer 80
Laycock, Benjamin F 1
Laycock, Norman A
Laytham, Frank 9
Leach, Errol William C 83
Leaver, James Michael T
Lee, Clifford 93
Leeming, Fred 126
Lees, Alfred 111
Leigh, Harry 87
Lewis, T J 68
Leyland, Arthur 12
Liggins, Thomas 84
Lightfoot, Norman 93
Lindsay, Frederick 75
Little, James R. 84
Livesey, Harry T
Lloyd, George Nelson A
Lloyd, Joseph 8
Lockett, John 49
Lockwood, Joseph Henry 12
Logan, Frederick 125
Lomax, Abel Thorpe 75
Longworth, William H P
Lonsdale, George P
Lonsdale, Richard A
Lord, Alfred T
Lord, Alfred H T
Lord, Joseph 92
Lord, Samuel T

Lord, William 93
Lott, John Cyprian 84
Lowe, James 44
Luckwell, Walter 126
Lund, Giles 93
Lyon, James Albert 1
Lyons, Herbert A
Lyons, John J 62

MacGrath, Andrew 121
Mainwaring, John D 62
Makin, Clifford 121
Makin, William PZ
Makinson, James 48
Mallinson, Charles H 81
Mantle, Joseph Henry A
Marsden, Frank T, P
Marsh, Absalom P
Marshall, Joseph 27
Marsland, Edmund T
Martin, James 53
Mason, William Y
Masser, Horace 35
Matthew, Wilfred 22
Mawdsley, James Henry 94
McCabe, James A
McCall, Samuel 62
McDonald, William P
McDonough, William 12
McGowan, John A
McGregor, Robert 138
McKee, Albert A
McKenna, Patrick A
McKenna, William B 94
McKenzie, Bernard F 12
McKernan, Francis J P
McMurray, Charles P
McNamara, Gilbert J P
McQuilliam, Frederick 126
McVeigh, Peter 12
Mercer, Albert T

Metcalf, John T
Milner, Daniel A
Milner, John Holden 12
Milton, George 30
Milton, William T
Mitchell, David 12
Mitchell, Henry H 89
Molloy, John 93
Moore, Arthur 105
Moore, James Oliver A
Moorhouse, James 12
Morgan, John A
Morgan, Michael 12
Morris, James Robert A
Morris, Joseph Cyril 67
Mortimer, William 12
Moss, Perry TC
Moulton, Samuel P
Muchmore, Thomas W 70
Mulhall, Albert T
Mulhall, James 93
Mulhall, Thomas 93
Mundy, Richard Henry 49
Murphy, John T
Murphy, Thomas A
Murray, Henry 12
Myers, Frank T
Myerscough, William 49

Nadin, Arthur A
Neal, Frank 24
Nicholls, Michael Henry 78
Nicholson, William A
Nickson, Edward T
Noble, John William T
Nolan, Joseph P
Norris, Harold 12
Nowell, John P
Nutt, Charles Edwin 28
Nutter, Arthur 18
Nutter, Harry T

O'Connor, John T
Ogden, John 84
O'Hare, William T
Ollett, Samuel P 1
O'Neill, Patrick P
Openshaw, Arthur 14
Orme, Frederick William A
Ormerod, Frank 21
Ormerod, Richard 49
Ormerod, William Arthur 94

Papworth, Charles 88
Parker, Harold A
Parker, Hubert 31
Parkington, Fred T
Parkinson, Edward T
Parkinson, William Henry 93
Parry, Thomas Owen T
Pate, William PZ
Pates, William H 84
Pawson, William 4
Pearson, John 66
Peel, Herbert S 93
Pemberton, Fred 92
Pemberton, Harold 21
Pendlebury, James T
Pendlebury, Richard 93
Pepper, Sydney 70
Perry, John William P
Pettie, Philip John 42
Pickering, John 44
Pickering, Robert 119
Pickering, William James 94
Pickles, Richard 4
Pickles, Robert F 119
Pickles, William 70
Pickup, Frederick 94
Pickup, George T
Pickup, John 113
Pickup, William P

Pickvance, Joseph 108
Pilkington, George W. 84
Pilkington, Harry 70
Pilkington, James Albert P
Pilling, Samuel T
Pincott, George Stanley P
Pitman, William A
Place, Ernest T
Plummer, Thomas 95
Podd, Benjamin G 63
Podmore, George D 90
Pollard, John T
Pollitt, James Henry 27
Pooley, John A
Power, Henry 11
Prendergast, John W 4
Prescott, Robert Stuart 15
Preston, John Joseph P
Price, Francis P
Pritchard, Thomas A
Proctor, Harry 93
Prothero, Thomas 126
Pull, Walter A
Pye, Andrew A

Quinn, Frank 84
Quinn, James 11

Radcliffe, Frederick W 42
Ralph, Joseph James 114
Ramsbottom, Ernest 9
Ratcliffe, William T
Rawcliffe, Herbert C T
Rawnsley, Ambrose 86
Rayton, Henry T
Redmond, Daniel 12
Rhodes, Albert 99
Rickman, Arthur W 134
Ridge, George 34
Riding, William A, A
Rigby, Henry 123

Rigby, William G M 56
Rigg, Albert T
Riley, Arthur 16
Riley, Ernest T
Riley, Henry Davison T
Riley, Joseph T
Riley, Matthew 91
Riley, Robert 30
Riley, Wilfrid 102
Riley, Willie T
Rimmer, Oliver T
Roberts, Fred 18
Roberts, James Henry 11
Robinson, Edgar John 4
Robinson, Thomas T, 63, 3
Robinson, William 12
Robinson, Willie T
Rodgers, Harold 84
Rodwell, Harry 93
Rogers, Albert Edward T
Rollins, Seth T
Rooney, Matthew 97
Roscoe, George A
Roscoe, James Joseph 126
Ross, Frederick Bruce 64
Rossall, William 118
Routh, Thomas 64
Rowe, Frank P
Rule, John Ernest L
Rushton, Harry Barton 4
Rushton, Joseph 111
Russell, John 93

Sanders, George T
Sanderson, Harry 12
Saunders, Harold M 64
Saunders, Leonard T
Searle, Charles A
Senior, John H P
Shambrook, Arthur A
Sharpe, William 49

Sharples, Joseph 25
Sharples, Richard 135
Shaw, Crowther T
Shaw, Samuel P
Sheffield, Frank 47
Shepherd, John A 5
Short, William 113
Shuttleworth, Edward T
Shuttleworth, John 130
Simm, William 12
Simms, James 26
Simpson, Harry 94
Singleton, Lawrence 44
Singleton, William 93
Slater, Joseph 12
Slater, Thomas P
Slinger, William 58
Smith, Edward 87
Smith, George Edward 77
Smith, Gilbert 46
Smith, James P
Smith, John 93, 31
Smith, Samuel 49
Smith, Thomas P
Smith, Walter 64
Smith, Wansey 66
Smith, William 9
Smithies, Robert T
Smithson, Robert 44
Smolenski, Charles P
Southworth, Robert 21
Speakman, James T
Spedding, Thomas T
Spencer, Alfred 71
Spencer, Frank 111
Squires, James T
Stacey, John 12
Stanger, Adolphus 14
Stansfield, Arthur 64
Stanton, Walter 136
Starkie, Albert P

Starkie, Earl 118
Stevenson, John 9
Steventon, A.T. 1
Stewart, John 118
Stockdale, John 4
Stonall, James Richard 87
Stonehouse, Charles T
Stones, Joseph 121
Storey, Bertram James A
Storey, Herbert 12
Stott, Frederick 94
Stott, William P
Strowger, Peter 125
Stuttard, George T
Sullivan, Daniel 10
Sunderland, Robert 63
Sunderland, Thomas A
Sunley, Walter T
Sutcliffe, James R 113
Sutcliffe, Walter T

Talbot, Joseph Thomas 93
Tarrant, Percival John 64
Taylor, Edgar 33
Taylor, Edwin Lomax P
Taylor, Fred P
Taylor, Guy Rawstron 125
Taylor, John 126
Taylor, Robert P
Taylor, Thomas T
Taylor, William A 106
Thomason, John William 109
Thompson, Herbert William T
Thompson, Isaac 126
Thompson, James Fairclough T
Thompson, Jerry T
Thompson, John 93, A
Thompson, Joseph A 80
Thornley, Ralph Hulme 49
Thornton, Henry 62
Thornton, Richard H 47
Thorpe, John Bramwell 113

Todd, Walter Counsell T
Tomlinson, William T
Tootell, William 93
Topping, John James 106
Torevell, Joseph Edward Y
Tough, Arnold B 93
Tristram, Edward A
Tuhey, James 49
Turner, Frederick John A
Turner, John William 12
Tuton, John Henry T
Tyrer, Albert A
Tyson, Arthur T

Unsworth, Herbert T
Uttley, Richard 93

Varley, William Henry 32
Veevers, Harold 31
Vickers, Matheas 28

Waddington, Harry P
Waddington, John 31
Wade, Frederick R 49
Wadsworth, John B T
Walkden, J W 39
Walmsley, Robert 126
Walsh, James 49, 4, 12
Walsh, Robert 44
Walton, Joseph A
Warburton, John A
Ward, James 41, 1
Ward, John Edward T
Ward, Walter A
Wardleworth, Vincent E 36
Washbrook, Mark Thomas 121
Watmough, Richard 12
Watson, Harry T
Watson, James Allan 49
Watson, Sydney 103
Wayland, Richard B. 26
Webb, Frederick T

Webster, Harry 105
Westwell, Fred T
Whalley, Joseph T
Whewell, Frederick A
Whewell, Herbert T
Whitchelo, Robert W A
White, George P
White, Wilfred 12
Whitehead, Albert 76
Whittaker, Earl A
Whittaker, Jacob 2
Whittaker, Thomas 18
Whittaker, William 12
Widdop, Clarence 106
Wighton, George Edwin 113
Wignall, James 116
Wild, James Edward A
Wildman, Cecil 12
Wilken, Edmund H P
Wilkinson, Albert T
Wilkinson, Fred T
Wilkinson, Harold 39
Wilkinson, William 26
Williams, George G 47
Williams, Harold Stanley 65
Williams, Thomas 87
Wilson, John 121
Wilson, Rennie 70
Wilson, Robin 84
Winchester, Thomas W 4
Winder, Harold 4
Winter, John 104
Wixted, James Clarance H
Wixted, John T
Wolstencroft, Joseph 98
Wood, Herbert T
Woods, James Henry 12
Woods, Stephen 100
Woolfenden, James P
Wray, William George 93
Wright, Thomas 64

Wright, William P

Yates, Thomas 18
Yates, Thomas Henry T
Young, David 18
Young, John T

AN INDEX OF PRINCIPAL PLACES MENTIONED IN THE TEXT

Memorials: